rec'd 9-26-17 ⅀15.20

$1.25

U.S. CAMERA INTERNATIONAL PICTURES 1965

Edited by Tom Maloney

PHOTOGRAPH BY WILLIAM CADGE

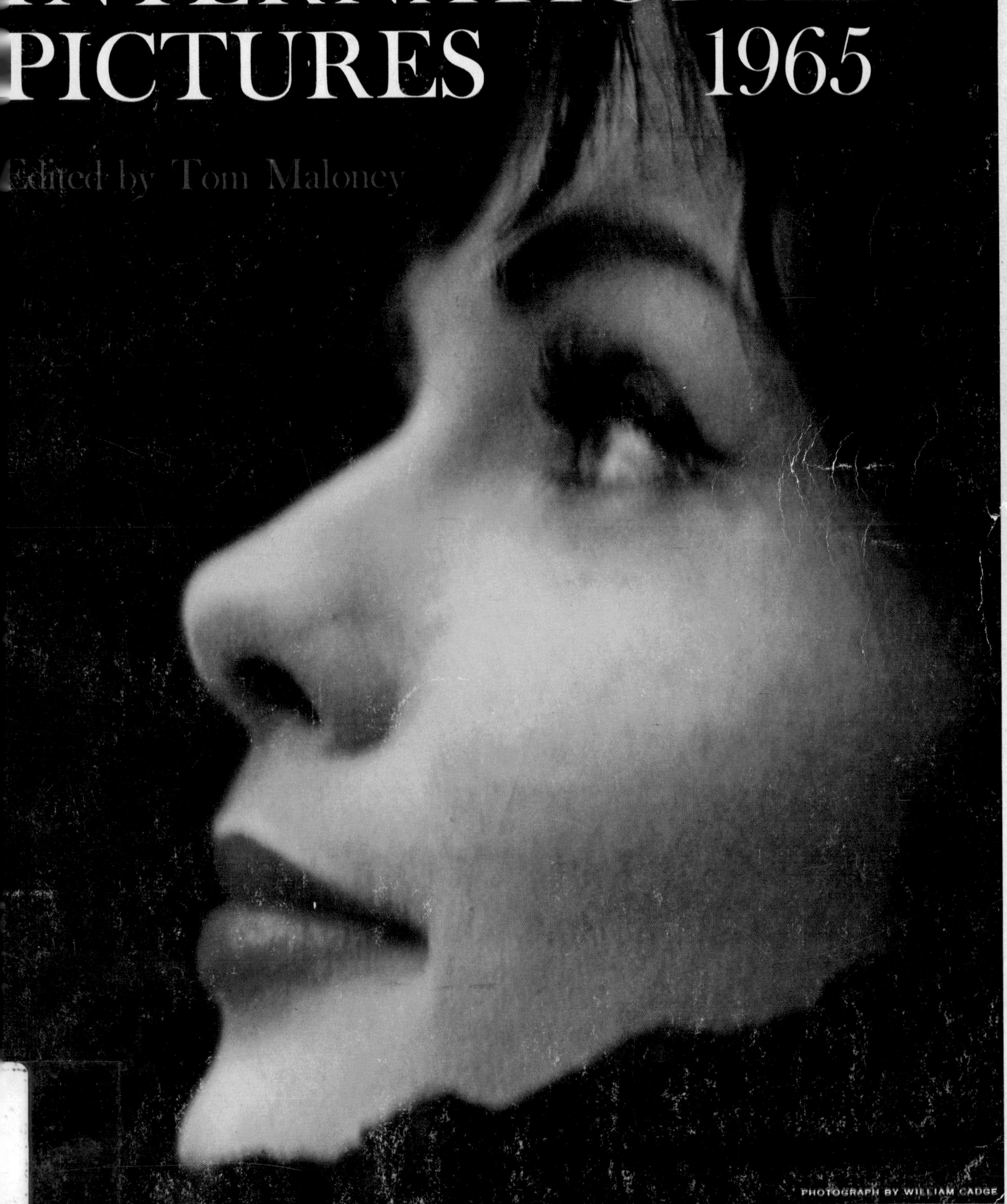

Today...Mathew Brady would probably have used a Nikon

(most pros do!)*

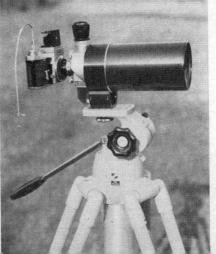

U. S. CAMERA
INTERNATIONAL
PICTURES 1965

Edited by TOM MALONEY

ASSOCIATE EDITORS

MARY P. R. THOMAS · JACK L. TERRACCIANO

*DEEP IN Connecticut
country the great pho-
tographer Edward Stei-
chen, now eighty-four
years of age, takes in
the flag at sundown on
his farm.*

Bruce Davidson

CONTENTS

STEICHEN TALKING

ABOUT PHOTOGRAPHY, PEOPLE, FREEDOM

EXCERPTS FROM "A LIFE IN PHOTOGRAPHY," A NEW AUTOBIOGRAPHY BY EDWARD STEICHEN

"...It takes a powerful generative force to produce a work of art in any medium...."

"...The most damaging restrictions on an artist's liberty are self-imposed. So often, what may have begun as fresh thinking and discovery is turned into a routine and reduced to mere habit...."

"...My first real effort in photography was to make photographs that were useful. And, as I look back over the many intervening years, I find that usefulness has always been attractive in the art of photography...."

"...The artist, in any medium, does not live in a vacuum. There is a relationship between everything that is being done and everything that has been done before...."

"...While the artist working in any other medium begins with a blank surface and gradually brings his conception into being, the photographer is the only imagemaker who begins with the picture completed. His emotions, his knowledge, and his native talent are brought into focus and fixed beyond recall the moment the shutter of his camera has closed...."

"...Destructive loss of freedom comes from an overflow of egoism, when the ego spills over and expresses itself as conceit...."

"...Excessive humility can also be a weakness impinging on freedom, but in every great artist humility is always an important part of his attitude toward nature and toward his medium. This kind of humility opens doors and vistas, whereas conceit shuts them tight...."

"...A portrait must get beyond the almost universal self-consciousness that people have before the camera.... The essential thing was to awaken a genuine response...."

"...I came to the conclusion that I had been working from a negative approach, that what was needed was a positive statement on what a wonderful thing life was, how marvellous people were, and, above all, how alike people were in all parts of the world...."

"...When a certain set of habits become general, a whole art period can condemn itself to the loss of freedom...."

"...When an artist of any kind looks at his subject, he looks with everything he is. Everything that he has lived, learned, observed, and experienced combines to enable him to identify himself with the subject and look with insight, perception, imagination, and understanding...."

"...Photography is a medium of formidable contradictions. It is both ridiculously easy and almost impossibly difficult...."

"...The people in the audience looked at the pictures [in *The Family of Man*], and the people in the pictures looked back at them. They recognized each other. A Japanese poet has said that, when you look into a mirror, you do not see your reflection, your reflection sees you...."

"...To imagine that a visual artist in any medium could condense a complete portrait into one picture is putting a strain on logic. Every human being has the capacity for both laughter and tears, and there is no point halfway between that combines the infinite range of human complexities and contradictory states of heart and mind involved in the human condition...."

"...Freedom is something that is in the air of a country...."

NEAR THE WATER'S bank, where Steichen's favorite shad-blow tree grows, Mr. and Mrs. Edward Steichen spend a few leisure hours rowing.

Bruce Davidson

ON CAMERA—THE MOON

The flight of Ranger 7, which took some 4,000 close-range photographs of the moon before crash landing on its surface, gave a tremendous boost to the entire U.S. space program. In Washington, D.C., President Johnson (above) looks at a moon picture shown to him by Dr. William Pickering of the Jet Propulsion Laboratory of Pasadena, Calif. The scientist told the President the Sea of Clouds would be an ideal spot for landing a manned spaceship. The six television cameras (seen below) and a supporting communications system were the payload of the Ranger 7 spacecraft which the National Aeronautics and Space Administration rocketed to the moon. Designed and built for the Ranger probe by the Radio Corp. of America, the camera system yielded the first close-up photos of the lunar surface. The two middle cameras (top and bottom) transmit at the rate of one full-scan picture every 2½ seconds. The four outer cameras, being more than 12 times faster, send back one partial-scan (and thus slightly smaller) picture every 2/10 seconds. U.S. scientists heralded the photographs which showed craters as small as three feet wide. The thousands of pictures of the lunar surface, a thousand times clearer than ever before, climaxed one of the most successful space missions in history.

THE ENTIRE picture-taking apparatus, which included 2 radio transmitters, was made by RCA of America, weight 382 lbs.

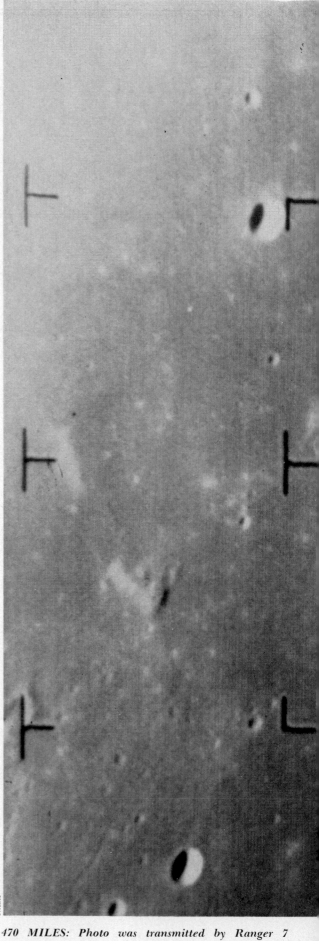

470 MILES: Photo was transmitted by Ranger 7

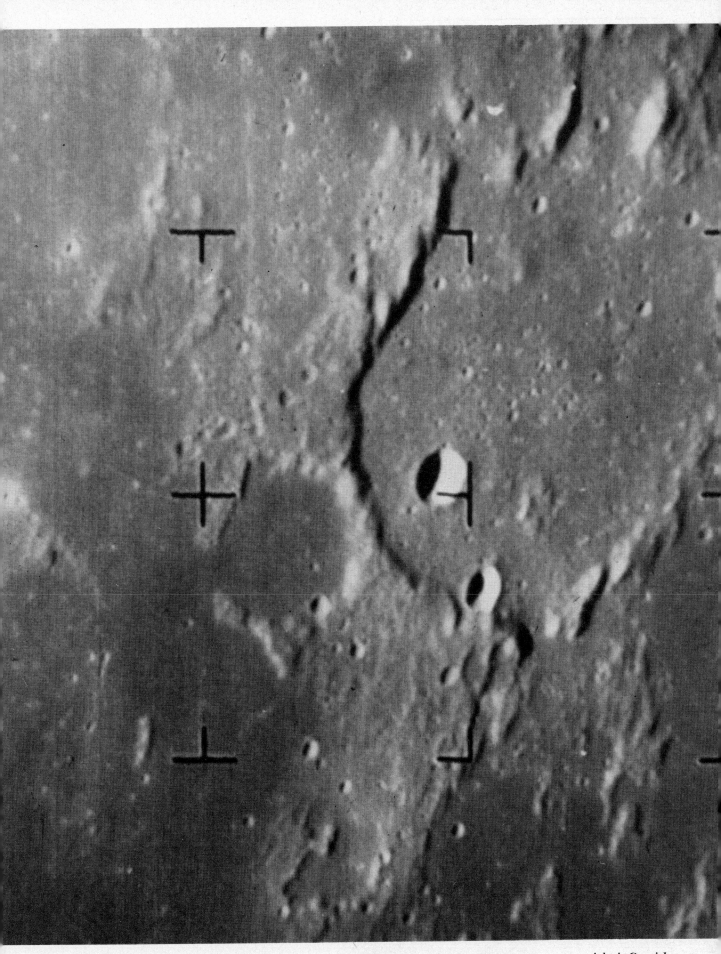

when it was 470 mi. from the moon and shows an area about 75 mi. on each side. Large crater at upper right is Guericke.

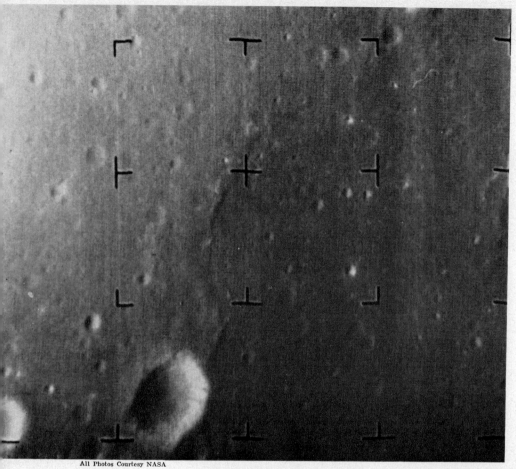

All Photos Courtesy NASA

25 MILES: Now the smaller craters are just 50 feet in diameter and it can be seen that some have steep sides, others shallow. Ranger TV has nearly triple the detail of a home television screen.

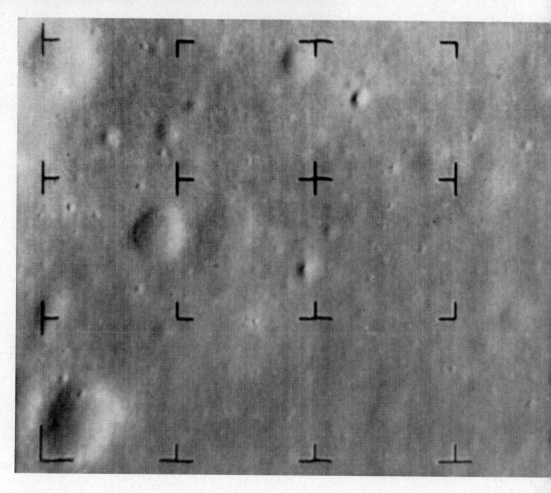

8 MILES: And here the smallest craters perceptible are but 25 feet in diameter. The area shown is about 2.7 miles on a side. Views were far better than scientists expected. Fine spacing of TV lines give pictures the quality of good photographs.

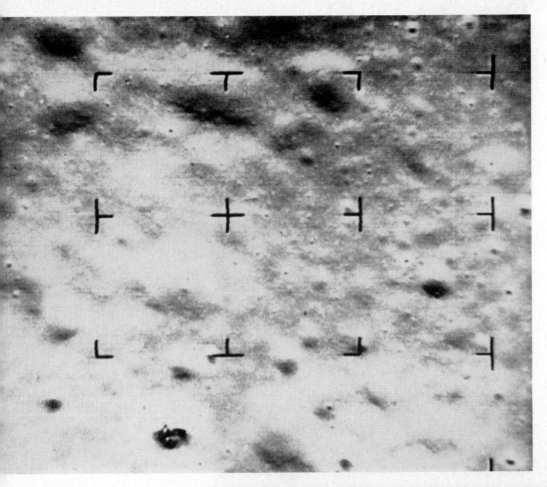

3 MILES: As the Rang-
er 7 spacecraft nears its
death, all the cameras
are still working per-
fectly. This area is one
and two-thirds miles
square. Cameras were
shooting twenty-five to
three-hundred photo-
graphs per minute.

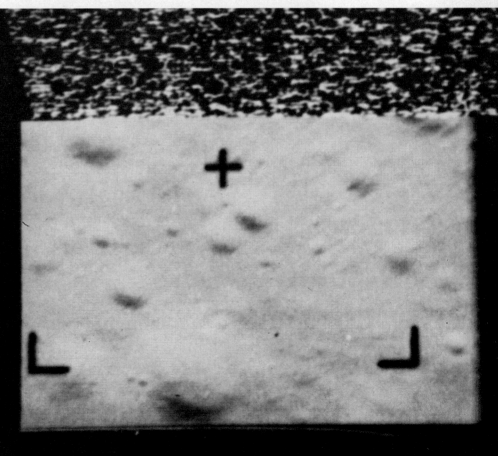

*3,000 FEET: This last view
ended in transmitter noise as
the Ranger crashed and the
scanner stopped. Photo readers
could distinguish craters three
feet across and one foot deep.*

11

SUZY PARKER
PHOTOGRAPHED BY BERT STERN

One of the most dramatic and most talked of series of photographs to be taken, during the 1964 fashion year, were Bert Stern's outrageously beautiful and dazzlingly sexy pictures of Suzy Parker, pictured in a variety of spicy swimsuits. Eight of them originally appeared in *McCall's* magazine and four of them have been "lifted" for viewing here.

Contrary to belief, Stern has not photographed Suzy all that much. Except for brief editorial forays, the *McCall's* assignment was the first chance they had to really spend some time with each other.

Stern recalls that she is great fun to work with and to photograph; when he told her that he was deliberately going to make her appear quite sexy in the new bare bathing suits, she just laughed, was not really convinced. But, after the shooting started, she fell in immediately with the idea—you can judge the results for yourself. She has an extraordinary passion to be better than anyone else at whatever she does and she adores being photographed. When she saw the finished pictures, she was terribly pleased and called Bert to tell him so.

Whether in color or black and white, Suzy Parker bowls the viewer over with her classic construction of beauty. She is a bundle of animation, enthusiasm, anticipation and integrity. For those interested in seeing Miss Parker in black and white, we have chosen four photographs for your selective eye, some of them were taken on assignment for *Vogue*. Incidentally, Georgia is pictured with her famous mother on page 14.

Suzy Parker, now Mrs. Bradford Dillman, lives with her handsome actor husband and four-year-old daughter Georgia de la Salle, by a former marriage, in New York, a city she loves.

It was inevitable that the combination of Miss Parker and Mr. Stern would touch off a photographic explosion. Both have been in the spotlight from the beginning of their careers; one of the great model personalities of her time, Suzy Parker's earnings are reputed to run in the six figures and Bert Stern may well be the best working photographer in New York.

BERT STERN   17

BERT STERN

BERT STERN

ANDREAS FEININGER

EDITOR'S NOTE: One of America's most distinguished men with a camera is Andreas Feininger. His book, The World Through My Eyes, *reveals anew Feininger's imaginative way of looking at form and substance, at nature and man. Through his eyes the world is indeed a wide and wonderful place. On these pages we present too few pictures from this magnificent book along with the captions. As an added bonus, we have reprinted four chapters exactly as they appear in the book, in which the author shares with the reader his ideas and reflections, his methods, and the philosophy that photography is truly a language in itself.*

Pictures cover every available space in my workroom—the walls, the floor, chairs, tabletops. They are placed for review: a selection from the accumulation of twenty-five years, spread out so that I can examine what I have done during that time. I want to see how far I succeeded in conveying my own feeling about a subject, in presenting an idea.

No one can evaluate his own work with complete objectivity, no matter how honest his intention. But one tries. And faced with this massive collection of prints, I asked myself a question: Have I fulfilled what I set out to do, and if so, has my initial intention not only been present but present in an aesthetic frame? Are the pictures striking enough that, seen again in such number, they still are interesting? Are they sufficiently interesting that the observer, finding some new appreciation through them and remembering them, is made more aware or more thoughtful?

And looking at these pictures, I considered these things and thought about my beginnings as a photographer and what had made me choose photography as a profession.

In my youth I dreamed of becoming a scientist. I roamed the fields and woods surrounding my home town, observing and collecting animals and plants, wishing I could record them in

THE WORLD THROUGH MY EYES

their natural habitat. One Christmas I was given a camera. The first photograph I ever made was of crows feeding in a snow-covered field. In the print, the crows appeared as specks, so great was the distance between them and me. Perhaps it was this first failure to get the image I had imagined that accounted for my later interest in tele- and close-up photography.

When circumstances prevented me from pursuing a scientific career I became an architect. In the course of my studies I saw many buildings, constructions, and structural details that appealed to me. At first I started to sketch these, but I soon found that sketching was too slow and inaccurate. Instead, I began to photograph them, and I discovered the camera was an ideal means by which to compile a pictorial reference library of my own.

The political upheaval of the mid-thirties (I lived in Europe at that time) made it impossible for me to continue my career as an architect, and so I became an architectural photographer. Now I found myself taking pictures for other architects and the editors of architectural magazines.

When World War II began, I came to the United States and was fortunate enough to become a *Life* photographer. With that, the most exciting period of my career began. In working for *Life*, the thrill of traveling, meeting interesting people, getting into places barred to most others, and seeing things that I could not otherwise have seen at first hand was just as great as that of the photographic work. I was in the enviable position of doing what pleased me most and being paid for it by the magazine. And since my assignment editor, Wilson Hicks, was very much aware that any photographer does his best work if a subject has interest for him, most of my assignments involved things I loved—the objects and forms of nature, and the works of man.

Paradoxical as it may sound, I ascribe whatever success I have had in photography to the fact that my greatest interest has always been in the subjects of my pictures, not in photographic equipment and technique. In fact, I was so little concerned by the mechanics of picture-making that I never bothered to learn in the approved manner by being apprenticed to a photographer or by attending a photo school. Instead, I carefully read and conscientiously tried to follow the instructions that accompanied any camera, film, or developer I bought. Of course, I made mistakes I might have avoided if I had had proper guidance. However, being a perfectionist by nature, when I was dissatisfied with what I had produced, I stubbornly looked for the cause of the trouble, and if I succeeded in finding it, I rarely made the same mistake again. As a result of this self-education, I acquired a thorough understanding of the entire photographic process which I doubt I would have obtained by any other method.

Interest in a subject gives the necessary spark that is required for anyone's best work. It is interest that stimulates the desire to explore one's theme, and it is in such exploration that a photographer often makes unexpected discoveries or gains the insight without which he could not have made a meaningful photograph.

Part of the reward one receives for his work is the knowledge that it will be seen and appreciated by others; part of its meaning is the meaning beyond oneself. And photography provides a universal method of communication, breaking through the barriers of language so easily that no barriers seem to exist. At this perilous time in our world, communication and understanding are vitally important, so photography should rank high as an avenue of international intercourse.

To me, the camera is a tool that serves many purposes. It is there when I find subjects which I am compelled to photograph—to record them for my own study or enjoyment; it is there when I want to photograph for others what has appealed to me, so that I can share what I think important or beautiful.

Though the approach of photographers may range from the objective to the subjective, and their pictures appear very different, good pictures have at least one common factor—interest. The way in which each photographer chooses to work is almost always determined by his interest.

In the objective approach, the photographer tries to efface himself, to record the subject as faithfully as possible, presenting it to the observer for his own interpretation. This is the approach of the scientist or documentarian. It is the technique I most often follow. Two

others who have used this approach at its highest level are Cartier-Bresson and Edward Weston. In the subjective approach, a photographer's feelings are engaged. He wants us to be drawn by his own reaction, to feel as he felt. If his insight and creative ability are of a high order, he catches us in his net. We see as he has seen, in the depicted intensity of his own vision. And once caught, we are not captive, but released spontaneously to a wider view. Erwin Blumenfeld, Ernst Haas, and Gordon Parks are, in my opinion, outstanding photographers who follow a subjective approach in their work.

This, I think, is the greatest difference between the two approaches: In the first, the viewer's reaction is unprompted and he is thrown back to his own experience for reference. In the second, he is propelled toward the reaction of the photographer. As I have already said, I use the objective rather than the subjective approach to photography. I am fortunate enough to have a talent for analysis and organization, and I am primarily an observer. Since my mind inclines toward the scientific, my approach, as a result, is more intellectual than emotional. These qualities are, of course, reflected in my selection of subjects and in the form of their rendition.

Subjects I am most interested in primarily involve fact rather than feeling: the documentation of things rather than emotions. These subjects include manifestations of nature—rocks, plants, and animals in all their infinite variations—and the works of man. What interests me most in these subjects are the aspects of structure, function, and form. There is a functional beauty in all natural forms, and I feel strongly that only when man-made forms are related to their functions can the result be aesthetically satisfying.

Since I am primarily concerned with function and form, factors such as sharpness, contrast, and simplicity of com- (Continued on page 200)

THE FENCER. *En garde*—statuesque outward calm at the instant of highest tension, just before the duel starts.

The Female Form

There seems very little doubt woman is the oldest subject of the timeless compulsion that drives man to express concepts of importance in tangible form. It is not surprising that photographers, too, feel this same compulsion. Yet though they often try to express a concept through portrayal of the female form, they are usually unsuccessful. The main reason for their failure seems to lie in the fact that these images, although semiabstract insofar as they lack three-dimensionality, color, motion, and life, are nevertheless too realistic to represent a universal concept—the nude remaining a woman without clothes rather than becoming a figure that symbolizes womanhood.

I also have photographed the female nude, and in doing so, tried to apply to my photographs what I have learned from contemplating good sculpture of the female form. A good sculptor deliberately eliminates nonessential detail, de-personalizes the human form, and through simplification and abstraction brings out universal aspects. It is in this respect that most photographs of nudes fail—they are too anatomically correct, too detailed, too representative of one woman to take the mind of the observer beyond that particular form to those universal aspects of femininity that include such timeless concepts as beauty, love, fertility, motherhood, and the mysteries of birth and death.

When I photograph the nude I have to rely on techniques that are basically alien to my way of working: I deliberately offset, if not destroy, the ability of the lens to record minute detail with utmost precision. However, I achieve this, *not* by retouching the negatives or prints or otherwise subjecting them to alien techniques, but by using typically photographic means: strong light and deep shadows; outline and silhouette; and the "graphic" techniques of bas-relief, reticulation, and solarization.

Included in this section are a number of photographs of female nudes taken from my book *Maids, Madonnas, and Witches—Women in Sculpture from Prehistoric Times to Picasso*. In these photographs, my approach had to be quite different, since the essential work of abstraction had already been done by the sculptor. My task, as I saw it, was to bring out and to interpret, in terms of black and white, the artist's intent as embodied in the original.

This involved giving the most careful consideration to factors such as angle of view (a sculpture—a form in the round—presents an infinite number of different angles from which usually only one view can be chosen) ; illumination (the wrong type of light and the wrong type of shadows can falsify, even totally destroy, the effect of any sculpture) ; cropping (since a two-dimensional photograph and a three-dimensional sculpture are two completely different things, I believe that to achieve the strongest effect it is not only permissible, but often necessary, to limit the rendition to only part of the sculpture; to crop the image in the negative) ; and contrast control in the print (to amplify and complement the task of the illumination) .

SOLARIZED PRINT. In contrast to the boldness of bas-relief renditions, which is reminiscent of woodcuts, solarized prints suggest the elegance of engravings. Lines of often incredible delicacy form the boundaries of empty space, while interpenetration of positive and negative picture elements further strengthens the feeling of mystery and unreality.

The Undistorted Space

The concept of perspective is inseparably linked to that of distortion. For example, the more abruptly actual parallel lines appear to converge in a photograph, the stronger the impression of depth —an effect well illustrated by many wide-angle photographs. Such convergence is of course a distortion of reality, since the lines were truly parallel. Similarly, the smaller that an object of known dimensions is rendered in a photograph in relation to another object, the greater the distance in depth between the two appears to be. But this illusion of depth—the result of diminution, another manifestation of perspective—is likewise based upon distortion. It occurs even if the object rendered as the smaller of the two is in reality much larger than the object that appears large in the photograph. For instance, a distant building or mountain would appear much smaller in a photograph than a person close to the camera, and in this reversal of size, reality is rendered "distorted."

Normally, we accept a certain degree of distortion —convergence and diminution—in photographs, but in some we object to it. Although the laws of perspective apply in the vertical plane as well as in the horizontal or any other plane, in photographs of buildings, for example, the upward convergence of vertical lines—lines that are actually parallel—is usually felt to be a distortion of reality and rejected as a fault. For this reason, in photographs of buildings, interiors, furniture, and many closeups of objects with parallel sides, we render verticals parallel to avoid the feeling of distortion, even though this involves "correcting" perspective by using the swings and tilts of a view camera.

Obviously, a conflict exists between two different, mutually exclusive objectives: if one wishes to create an illusion of depth in one's pictures, distortion must be used; but if one wishes the impressions he creates to conform as closely as possible to reality, then distortion must be suppressed.

I have been conscious of the conflict between distortion and depth on one side, and freedom from distortion and lack of depth on the other, ever since I became seriously interested in photography, and have given it much thought. I see this conflict as a choice: which is more important, the illusion of depth or the suppression of distortion? I prefer to avoid distortion—partly because I consider distortion a falsification, therefore something to be avoided; and partly because the illusion of depth in a photograph is not entirely dependent upon perspective and distortion but can be created through juxtaposition of dark foreground and light background or contrast between sharpness and unsharpness (selective focus), two means that do not involve distortion. Besides, complete elimination of distortion is not possible; hence, controlling it does not mean that one's photographs will be entirely devoid of the depth that it creates.

As any photographer knows, the shorter the relative focal length of the lens and the shorter the distance between subject and camera, the more pronounced the effects of perspective and diminution—i. e., of distortion—and vice versa. I have made use of this fact from the time that I took my first telephotographs in 1936 in Stockholm, by working as far as practicable with a lens of the longest focal length and photographing my subjects from the greatest distance that circumstances would permit, to keep my renditions as free from distortion as possible. The resulting tele-perspective is characterized by two qualities: in relation to one another, the true proportions of objects are largely preserved—i. e., small objects appear relatively small in the picture even when they were comparatively close to the camera, and large objects appear relatively large and dominant even when they were far away from the camera; and space appears strangely compressed. However, the apparent compression of space is only an optical illusion. This fact can be verified by making the following experiment: From an identical camera position, take two photographs of the same distant subject, one with a lens of standard focal length, the other with a telephoto lens. If you enlarge the negative taken with the lens of standard focal length *to the same scale* as the negative taken with the telephoto lens is enlarged (which, of course, involves a different degree of magnification), you will find that as far as perspective is concerned, the section from the standard negative corresponding to the area covered by the tele-negative will be identical to the tele-negative except in sharpness. If one print is superimposed upon the other they will be seen to register perfectly, thus proving their perspectives identical.

I find this typical telephoto perspective extraordinarily beautiful. Photographs containing it give a feeling of monumentality not found in any other type of rendition. Somehow, they seem more true than ordinary photographs, and that after all is not surprising, for they are closer to reality.

FIFTH AVENUE. New York at noon in July.

The Near and the Small

Some of the pleasantest and most exciting hours I have spent in photographing have been devoted to making close-ups. I never tire of studying small, interesting objects, getting closer and closer to them as I rack out the lens, watching their images grow on the groundglass and their blurred forms become sharp, and experiencing that indescribable fascination of seeing hitherto unseen wonders take shape before my eyes.

In addition to being an inexhaustible source of intellectual and aesthetic experience, close-up photography has a strictly practical attraction: it can be engaged in anywhere at any time with very little expenditure for equipment. All one needs is a lens of short focal length, a camera that has a groundglass and an extension bellows or tubes, a tripod, and a couple of photoflood lamps or speedlights. Subjects in endless variety can be found everywhere. Some of my favorite pictures are of things discovered in my own home or garden, like the frost pattern formed on a windowpane (page 67) or a spiderweb (page 72). I rarely take a walk without carrying a few glass vials or other little containers to hold small objects of nature that I may find and wish to study more closely with my camera. If one walks in the woods or fields or along the seashore, there are many things to be found—shells and snails, skeletons of fish, feathers, insects, spiders, caterpillars, seed pods or interesting seeds, crystals, and other natural forms—and the search for such things not only makes one look more intently at his surroundings but often pays rich dividends in the unexpected discovery of strange and beautiful objects.

Although I prefer to photograph whatever I find in its natural surroundings, this is not always possible. In such cases, I take my finds home and there try to duplicate their original setting. This usually is not too difficult, since the area that needs to be reconstructed for photographic purposes rarely exceeds half a square foot. I put live insects and caterpillars on their own food plants or leaves before photographing them, and often keep them for days and weeks to record their life cycles before I give them their freedom. I once spent the better part of a summer in this pleasant sort of work, doing a picture essay on insects for *Life;* thirty-two color photographs from this set were subsequently reproduced in *Living Insects of the World.*

Speaking of color photographs, I believe that renditions in color and in black and white are equally valid; neither is superior, and the choice between the two should, in my opinion, always be made in relation to the specific demands of the subject itself. Each medium offers certain advantages, each has certain limitations. A rendition in color is more naturalistic but more difficult to control than a rendition in black and white, which is more abstract and therefore more subject to control. Thus, in black and white, the photographer has more leeway to create specific impressions. Whenever the decision is left to me, I use color only if color is one of the outstanding qualities of the subject; unless color contributes decisively to its characterization, I prefer to work in black and white. I mention this consideration now because this is the first chapter in which color photographs are shown; here, as in subsequent chapters in this book in which color photographs appear, color was always a necessary picture element, a factor without which a particular photograph would have been less meaningful.

WEB OF the yellow garden spider

A Portfolio of North American Scenery

Perhaps no other country possesses a greater wealth of scenic beauty and more varied landscapes—mountains and plains; rivers, lakes, and forests; deserts and cultivated lands—than the United States. I know the forty-eight states of the continental United States well, for I have traveled and photographed extensively in all of them for more than twenty years.

In the following portfolio are assembled fourteen photographs of views in the United States and one in Canada that to me seem particularly typical. This collection is, of course, severely restricted. The scope of the subject is so vast that it could not be covered in a thousand pictures. Some of the most famous and familiar sights are not included for the reason that they are so well-known and have been photographed so often and well; repeating them here would take space better used for photographs of things not seen before or not seen in such form.

Many of the following pictures are, as scenic photographs go, close-ups, showing the essence of an entire landscape in the form of a grain elevator, a farm, or a pair of railroad tracks. Some are in color, but only when color was of primary importance. Despite their limited number, these few photographs show an immense variety of scenery, ranging from the tidal flats of Maryland to the icy heights of the Rockies, from a lonely farm in Indiana to the stainless steel, bronze, and glass skyscrapers of New York. Together, they give at least an indication of the colossus that is America.

A GRAIN ELEVATOR in Nebraska. Stout though badly cracked and patched, this grain elevator—symbol of the midwestern plains—has a pattern that might have inspired certain works of modern abstract art.

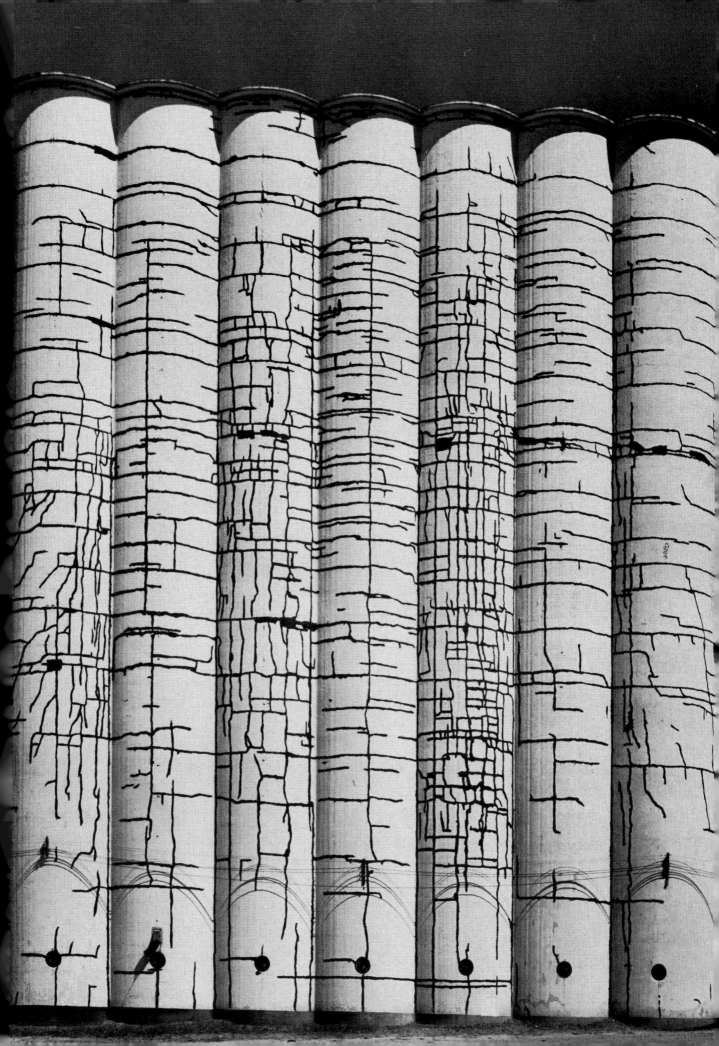

H. W. SILVESTER, *West Germany*

WYNN BULLOCK

A boy completely absorbed in catching a fish plus the added attractions of cracks in the sand, rotting pilings and reflections in the water are all part of Bullock's imaginative way of seeing. A man who never plans a photograph ahead of time, he took this visually strong and meaningful picture with an Ansco View 8x10 camera with a 14 inch lens. He exposed at 1/5th of a second at f/22. Super Hypan film. Daylight.

MATTHEW E. HARLIB

KARSH, *Ottawa*

Nikita Khrushchev

KARSH'S REPUTATION as a portrait photographer is unsurpassed. It has been his good fortune to meet the world's most distinguished men and women. And, in photographing them he has used the camera to portray them both as they appear to him, and, as they have impressed themselves on their generation. In April, 1963, Karsh journeyed to Russia where he made the portraits that appear on these four pages. Madame and Nikita Khrushchev at their country home. Lovely ballerina Svetlana Zakhvatoshina photographed at the Bolshoi Ballet. The great composer, Khatchaturian in Moscow. 8x10 View camera.

KARSH, *Ottawa*

Aram. Khatchaturian

BRETT WESTON

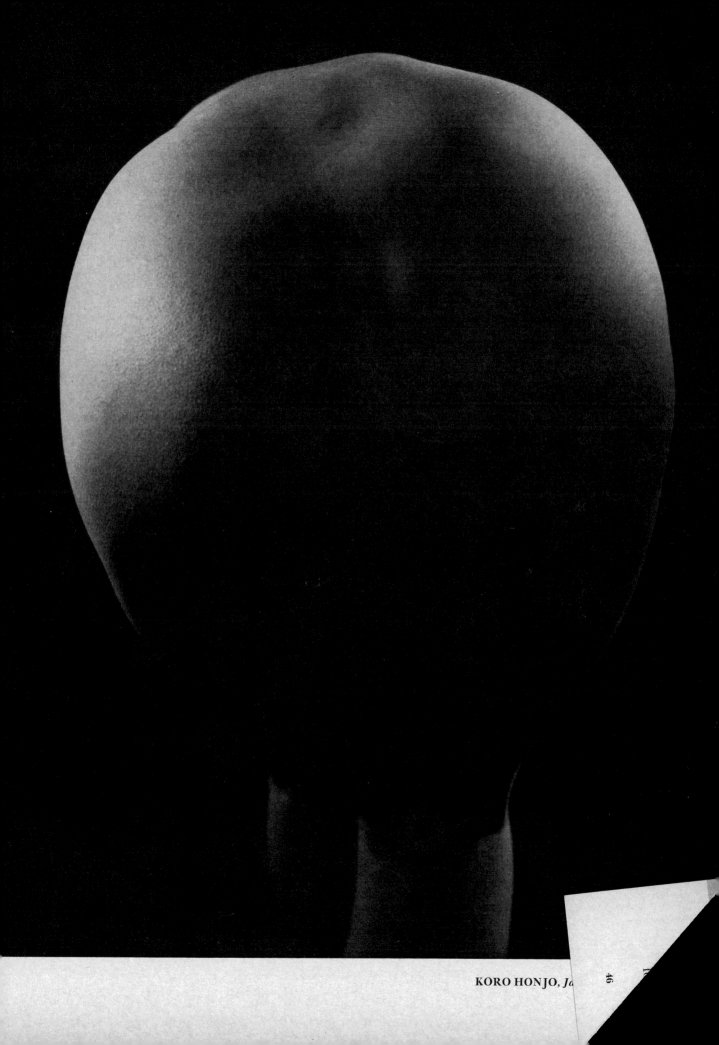

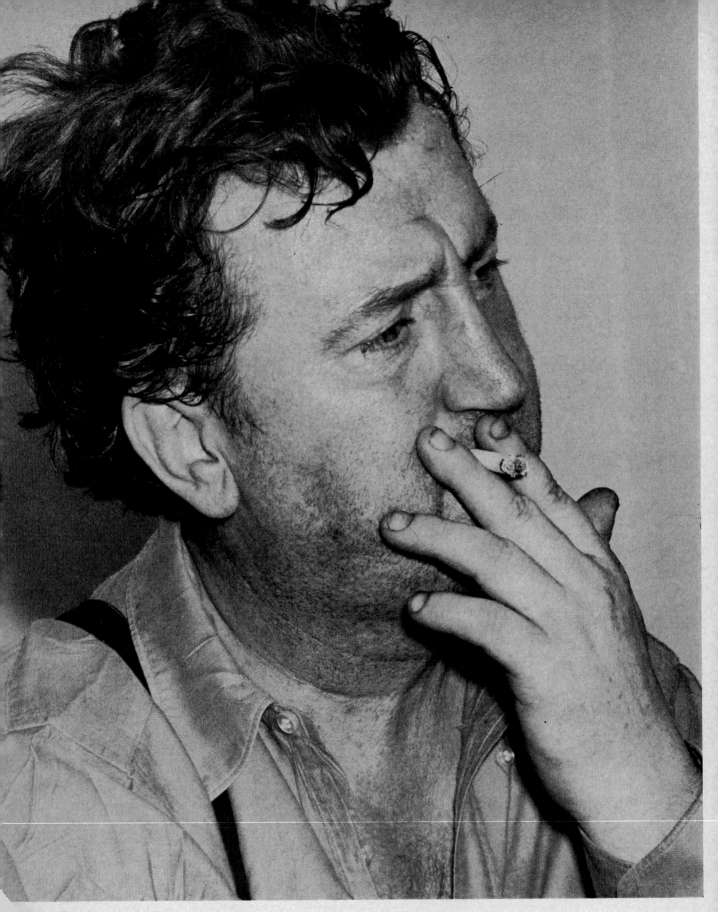

JAMES McANALLY, *Graphic House*

This picture of the late Irish man of letters is from a set of 30 shot in June, 1963 nine months before his death. They were made during a hot, humid afternoon in his rooms at the Chelsea Hotel in N.Y. during his last stay in the city. Leica M3, 135mm lens. 1/50 of a sec. at f/11. Speedlight, Plus-X.

GEORGES VIOLLON, *France (Both pages)*

A most successful free lance cameraman, Viollon taught himself the techniques of photography by reading books and magazines, visiting exhibitions and shooting, shooting, shooting. He prefers shooting out-of-doors and his favorite subjects are unposed. In Turkey he made this photo of a fruit store with the clerk standing on the sidewalk. He used a Leica 3f camera and exposed at 1/100 at f/11. The silver shop, opposite page, was taken in Yugoslavia. The store front without the man would have been just another picture. Viollon waited until the owner lounged in the doorway adding to the photo a more personal meaning. He again used a Leica 3f camera. Exposure was 1/100th of a second at f/8.

◀ **AD WINDIG,** *Holland (Page 47)*

While in the Congo in Central Africa, Windig made this photograph of a smiling native girl. Her attitude and pose give this figure study a wonderful feeling of innocence, beauty and simplicity. Windig used a Rolleiflex with a Xenar 3.5 lens. He exposed at 1/200th of a second at f/11, shot on Kodak Pan X.

JAMES McANALLY, *Graphic House (Pages 50 and 51)* ▶

The use of a long lens atop a nearby hill pulled the background of the town of Segovia in close behind the church of the Vera Cruz, thereby creating an effective composition. Leica M3. The village of Al Mazaraah with its terraced field and olive groves is one of the visual joys of mountainous Lebanon. Rollei.

apid, communicative, Mark Shaw is a photographer who is clearly convinced of his own methods and ideas. His quick decisive intelligence, which is part of his charm, is one of the many reasons for his continuing extraordinary success.

The photograph of Charles Laughton (pages 56 and 57) was not posed, was not done on assignment and has never been published before. "It was taken for me," says Shaw. "I was shooting on the movie set of *Advise and Consent*. It was between takes on a very hot day and he was exhausted, so, he just sat there trying to get into the mood or whatever."

Mark Shaw feels that his best pictures are taken in just this way and refers to most of his photographs as "snapshots." "Pictures in general are like snapshots," he says, "the ease in which you shoot, the areas in which you can work and the lack of pretension—the whole point being, that it is easier for me to show a person as they really are—either by a characteristic gesture, a movement or a feeling. If you can get that, then your picture is successful. I sometimes feel that some of my worst photographs are made in the studio, but then you can't do what you want all the time. Most of my work that appears here is really just snapshots—Otto Preminger playing with his children, certainly is."

When he photographs, Mark Shaw purposely shoots with a minimum of movement and a minimum of pictures. "People tend to freeze in front of a camera," says Shaw. "I shoot a few frames and try not to move around too much in the room, it makes the person less aware of the photographer. Mainly, I try not to irritate but rather create an atmosphere of a friend taking their picture, rather than a professional. And, I do not believe in crazy angles. I don't want anyone to feel uneasy; that they are being photographed by some guy who is determined to come up with something *different*."

Photography has many levels, Mark Shaw sits on the top one. He is better today than he was yesterday and he'll be better tomorrow than he was today.

MARK SHAW

Victoria, Mark and Otto Preminger

◄ **MARK SHAW**

Charles Laughton

MARK SHAW

Melina Mecouri
MARK SHAW

PHILIPP GIEGEL, *Switzerland*
For the past several years one of the most popular yearly events is the International Balloon Sports Meeting held in Murren, with participants from most parts of the world. At the signal to go seven balloons took off and these two were photographed by Giegel from a sports airplane as they drifted over the Jungfrau area. Since 1949, Giegel has been the official staff photographer for the Swiss National Tourist Office. He made this dramatic shot with a Hasselblad 500C with a 250mm lens. He shot at 1/250th of a second at f/11 using Verichrome Pan film.

VITTORIO RONCONI, *Italy*
(Pages 62 and 63) ▶
Moved by the solitary meditation of these two sisters in white as they walked along the shore, Ronconi made this extraordinary picture with special emphasis on the heads, hands and feet. Rollei with a f/3.5 lens. Shot at 1/20th of a second at f/8. Shooting into the light, Ronconi made this remarkable photo of a "sea of nuns" as they marched beneath his second story window while attending the funeral of Cardinal Schuster of Milan. He used a Rolleiflex with a f/3.5 lens. The exposure was 1/60th of a second at f/8.

W. SUSCHITZKY, *England (Both pages)*

Suschitzky's superb markmanship in portrait photography is evidenced in these two pictures, Aldous Huxley, the late and great author and a beautiful Yemenite girl. She is a professional dancer who had a small part in a film made in Israel on which Suschitzky worked as cameraman. Both these truly sen-

sitive and penetrating images were made with a Hasselblad 500C camera using a 150mm lens. Ilford HP3 film. Lighting—photofloods and late evening sun. A constant contributor to *U.S. Camera*, one of his many cinema credits include Director of Photography for the movie, *The Small World of Sammy Lee.*

RENÉ-JACQUES, *France*

PHILIPP GIEGEL, *Switzerland*

WILLIAM CADGE

Willibm Cadge, a dark-haired, attractive young man with a quick affectionate smile has, in his short career, successfully combined photography with art direction. For the past four years he has been Art Director of *Redbook* magazine. Just before that he was an associate Art Director to Otto Storch at *McCall's* where, in 1959, he completely redesigned the format, type and visual concept of the magazine. It was at *Redbook* that he began to photograph professionally. His comments on his color follows.

Our covers are very realistic, believable people; mostly young women photographed with as much naturalism as possible and presented with as strong a cover design as taste will permit. A good magazine cover should be well designed and read fast, but the photograph should look relaxed and fresh.

The cover, for *International Pictures* 1965, was taken *after* a shooting session in the studio. It was taken outdoors in the rain—in so-called, bad light. It's this extreme immediacy of the medium that I find very exciting. Just any quick picture of a girl in the rain would not necessarily make a good cover. There has to be a quick awareness of natural circumstances that will compose on film into a story design.

The picture, opposite, of the little girl covering the kittens with her raincoat was taken to illustrate a fiction story. Many times in fiction illustration a photograph will catch the moment, mood, or feeling of a story better than a painting or a drawing.

I had taken pictures of our children and our neighbors children in different phases of eating for about a year. They were taken for my own amusement. The idea to use them to illustrate a children's food feature came later. If it had happened the other way around, I don't think the pictures would be as spontaneous. Pages 70 and 71.

The photograph of my wife and son in the window, page 72, was taken to illustrate an article. I wanted a sad, forlorn feeling. My background as a designer and painter helped immensely. The intense blue color was obtained by using High Speed Ektachrome Type B around sunset. The artificial light in the window being correctly color balanced for that film.

DAVE IWERKS *(Page 76)* ▶

This compelling and serenely beautiful portrait of the late Prime Minister Jawaharlal Nehru of India was made by Iwerks in Los Angeles on the morning of Nehru's 72nd birthday. Iwerks, who began his formal portraiture career in 1956, used a Sinar View camera, 210 Schneider Symmar lens. 1/10 of a sec. at f/16.

EDITH WORTH *(Page 77)* ▶

This shot of the Taj Mahal was taken by Edith Worth as she patiently waited for a sufficient number of turbaned heads to fill in the foreground. This would, she felt, convey the feeling of the famous structure. This unusual perspective of the much photographed monument proved well worth the wait. This picture was made last spring while on a trip around the world with her husband during which time they made two films on assignment for the American Friends Service Committee, one in Pakistan and one in Hong Kong. Leica camera with a 50mm lens. Exposure 1/100th of a second at f/16. Panatomic X.

JEAN SUQUET, *France (Both pages)*

A photographer will find a variety of means to emphasize compositional and design elements in a photograph. For instance, in his figure study of his wife, Sequet exaggerates the repetition of shapes through black and white contrast, giving the viewer a feeling of pleasure and harmony above and beyond the subject matter of the picture. For the picture below, Sequet waited until the youngster had reached a certain spot (on his journey homeward) to complete the picture's design. Both photos, Leica M3.

ROBERT LAWRENCE PASTNER

Of this picture of the sun setting over the Delaware Memorial Bridge, Pastner says: "I made this shot while driving home to New York City from a photographic trip to Ohio and Kentucky. I had crossed the bridge and looking back saw the clearly-defined sinking sun in just the right position to make an impact-filled picture. The circle of the sun repeated in the circle of the small lights in the arches, and the perspective of the arches leading the eye to the depth of the scene, made an exciting study in pattern and composition." Pastner, a specialist in magazine and editorial photography, has been widely published throughout the country. He made this shot with a Leica M3, 135mm lens. 1/250 of a second at f/8.

RICHARD MYRICK

Who could resist the temptation of photographing this contented baby hippo, especially if her name happened to be "Cuddles." She is only two months old and Myrick found her at the zoo in San Francisco. A photographer since 1947, after being given a miniature camera by his father, Myrick is mainly interested in photographing San Francisco, nature, animals and jazz musicians at work, though not necessarily in that order. He used a Mamiya single lens reflex camera with a 135mm lens to make this fun photograph. Exposure was 1/30th of a sec. at f/3.5 on Panatomic X film.

BERINGER & PAMPALUCHI, *Switzerland*

The glorious beauty of wintertime is felt in this snow scene in which the photographer deliberately placed the sun behind the trees to show the glisten-ing effect of the ice on the branches. The shadows in the foreground add to the composition. Hassel-blad with a light green filter. 1/100th at f/11.

DIMITRIOS HARISSIADIS, *Greece*

Squid may not be the most beautiful form of fish life but they certainly added dramatic impact to this picture. Harissiadis made this effective photo of drying squid in the fishing village of Skala Skamnia, on the island of Lesbos. Harissiadis, who was gathering photographic material for a picture book on the Grecian island, has been a photographer since World War II. He runs his own agency doing illustrative, publicity and technical photography. Rollei, 75mm lens. 1/125 of a sec. at f/11. Verichrome Pan.

WHO IS THAT?
by Robert Riger

EDITOR'S NOTE: Robert Riger, a mercurial outgoing artist and photographer, is the only journalist in America who has the ability to report with text, photographs and drawings. In 1963, he created and will continue to be responsible for, BEST PLAYS OF THE YEAR, *the 1st edition of the* only *pro football picture record of a single season in an American sport.*

When I returned to art school after the war I began to draw sporting events with a particular realism because that was the way I had seen them. In the thirties, I grew up over the Polo Grounds and watched top professionals play all year round. In my drawings I would imagine a scene in a game and draw it vividly and in great detail. I would "make it up" as the kids would say, but it would look very believable. I found, however, whenever I showed the finished drawing everyone would ask, "Who is that?" or "Who is he supposed to be?" I knew then if I were to do sports pictures, especially in this country, I could not just draw a composite anybody. If the picture were to have meaning or impact, it must be *somebody*.

The wide world of sport is total realism. It exists only because of the athlete. The game is superb because of one man. The man at the center of the drama. The one everyone asks about.

My dedication is to this man—the athlete. My work is a controlled, intensive involvement in his world without his knowledge of my being there; the total exploration of his business whether it be a quick sideline pass by a quarterback or a difficult corner at high speed by a racing car driver, or a blonde doing the 100-meter butterfly. I have a great inquisitiveness for information about what an athlete is doing and precisely how it is being done. After the war when the cameras and lenses improved I was forced to implement my draftsmanship with documentary photographs. I found the photographers were seeing more with their long lenses than I was. I added the dimension of photography purely for information. I never take a photograph as a photograph. I never pose a figure and never use lights. This direct approach combined with a considerable intelligence about each sport and many athletes did make me a photog- (Continued on page 202)

RAIN AND MUD and cold must be endured in a battle or in a game. The athlete trys to ignore the elements and plays although tactically, they may make a game inordinately close. As his defense recovers a fumble with 2 minutes remaining, Green Bay's Forrest Gregg, his head encrusted with mud, shouts triumphantly. This face reminded me of a massive head sculptured in clay by Rodin.

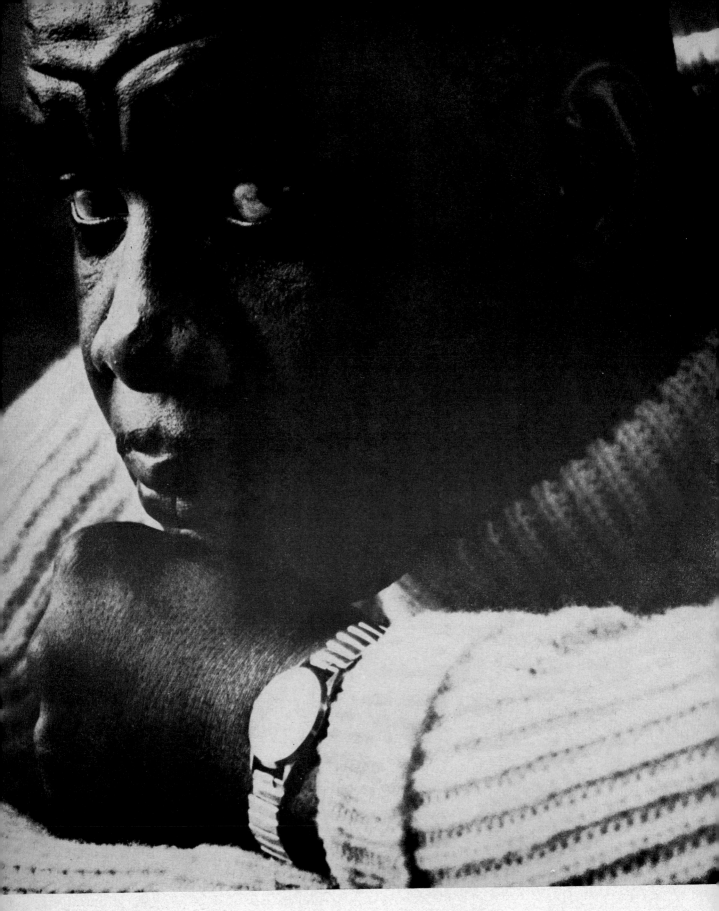

Robert Riger

THE CHARACTER of a man is in his eyes. Some men will kill you with a look while others will charm you with their laughter. Trapped in his training quarters when rain washed out a workout for his first fight with Patterson, Sonny Liston looks at the world. Willie Mays laughs with it.

Robert Riger

THE ATHLETE is not 24 years old forever—with a crew cut, a bronzed smooth face and 17" neck. Often he is much older, wiser, greying; masterful in the economy of his moves, elegant in stature—whether he's Antonio Ordonez killing a bull in Madrid, Stirling Moss listening to the British Anthem after his last Grand Prix victory in Monte Carlo, or Charley Conerly back on the bench after beating the Rams in his final year as a pro in N.Y. The great athletes of the world are quite the same.

Robert Riger

THE STAGE IS always set for the man but he is not always a star. In the early morning sunlight an ebullient exercise boy sits on top of his world—a million dollar horse—and forgets he's broke. You know how important the athlete is when the horse comes back empty and the jockey is lying somewhere up the track. Then the shock of his *not* being there is frightening.

ROBERT MONROE

An imaginative solution to a commercial assignment, in which the problem was to show changes in eye makeup, was this surrealistic effect created by taking two photographs and using them as one. Using a 4x5 view camera with a Schneider lens, Bob Monroe exposed at 1/2 second at f/11. Panatomic X film.

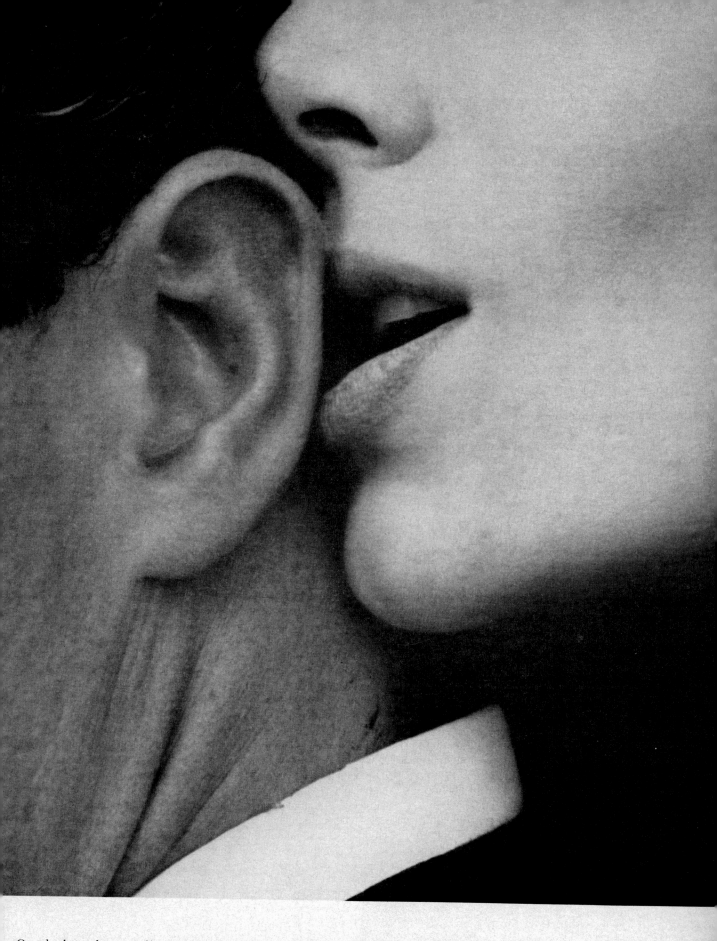

One look at the copy line, "It brings out the Tigress in you," brought out Robert Monroe's rich flair for interpretation clearly illustrated in this enticing shot —one of a series done for a perfume presentation. Camera used, Nikon F. Exposure was 1/30th of a second at f/5.6. Panatomic X film.

◀ **CARL FRANK** *(Page 92)*

As they leave the market place in Marrekech, after receiving their week's ration of wheat, the women of Morocco become walking advertisements for American aid to that country. For the balanced bags set upon their heads are clearly stamped: FURNISHED BY THE PEOPLE OF THE UNITED STATES OF AMERICA. Carl Frank made this photo with a Canonflex, exposed on Plus X film.

◀ **DAVE IWERKS** *(Page 93)*

In one terrible swift moment last November, John Fitzgerald Kennedy was assassinated in his 46th year. This sensitive portrait of the late President was taken four years ago by Iwerks during the Presidential campaign. Of it Iwerks says: "After the sitting, my impression was that he probably would become President. He was reserved, yet quite warm and also in a hurry to accomplish everything that was planned for the day." Camera, Graphic View with a 210mm Schneider Symmar lens. Exp. 1/10th of a sec. at f/16, Royal Pan film.

MARIO GIACOMELLI

This photo is one from a series that Giacomelli did on the Italian town of Scanno, all of which are now hanging in a gallery in Milan. Taken at 6 AM, Giacomelli was surprised to see a young boy playing at that time of morning. He made him the center of attention by using the old women of the town as composition material. A Kobell camera was used with a 105mm Heliar lens. The shutter speed 1/25th of a sec. f/5.6.

GEORGE W. MARTIN *(Pages 96 and 97)* ▶

George Martin thinks out every picture before taking it; the rest happens in the darkroom. He composes as thoroughly as he can before snapping the shutter but knows in advance that the composition will be completed in the darkroom. These two fine and carefully composed portrayals of the human form were made with a Nikon F, 35mm lens. Exposure 1/125th of a sec. at f/5.6. Plus X film.

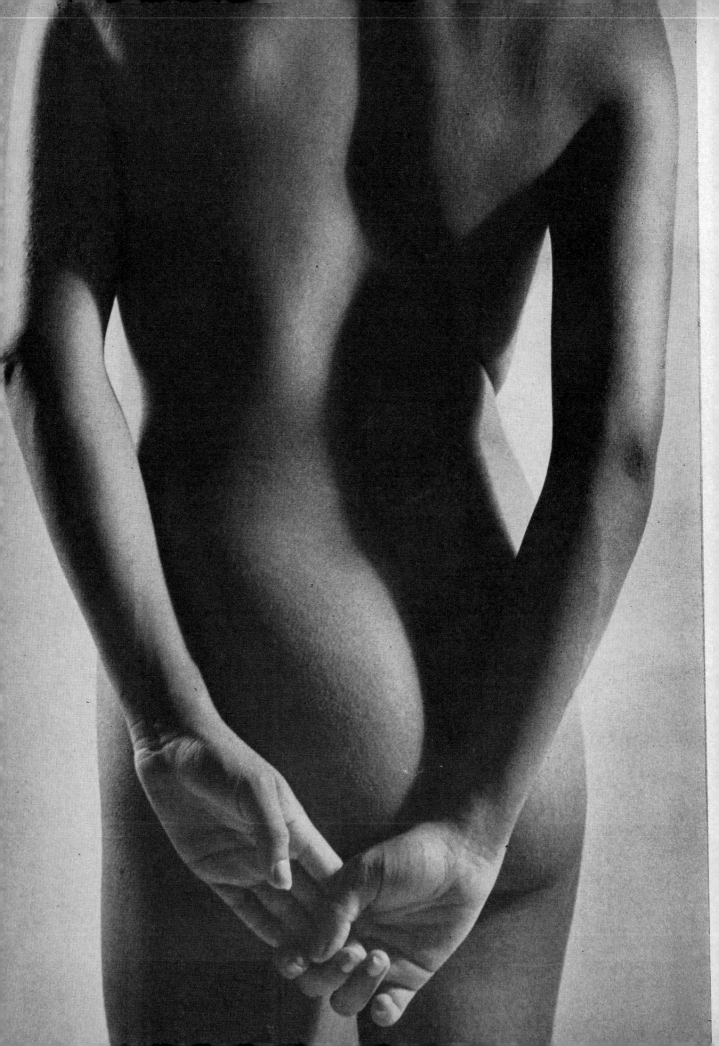

ATHANASIOS TSAGRIS, *Greece*

RENE JACQUES, *France* (Page 100) ▶

TODD WEBB (Page 101) ▶

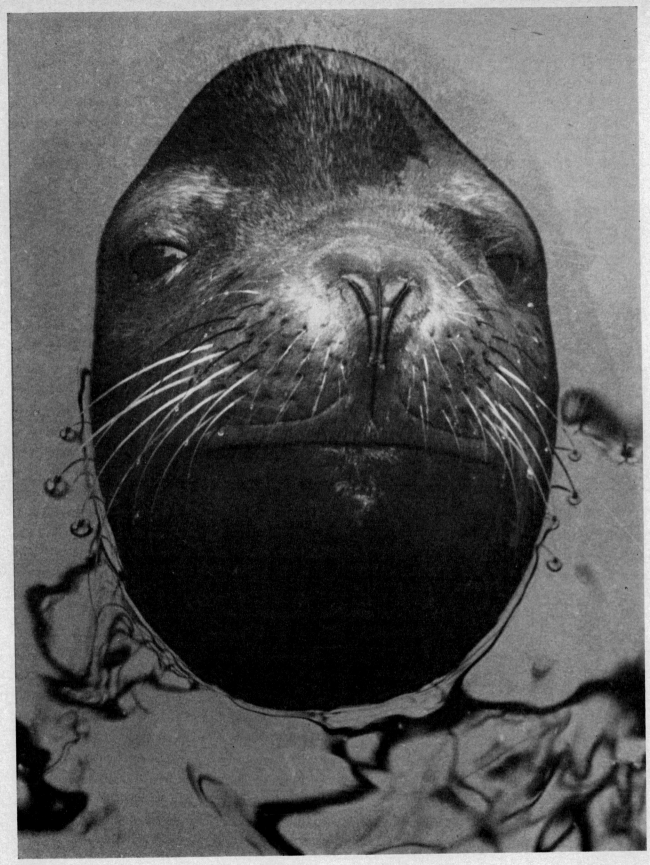

SHOSUKE YAMAGUCHI, *Japan*

ALFRED GESCHEIDT ▶

102

HASSE HANSON, *Sweden* (*Both pages*)

JEANLOUP SIEFF

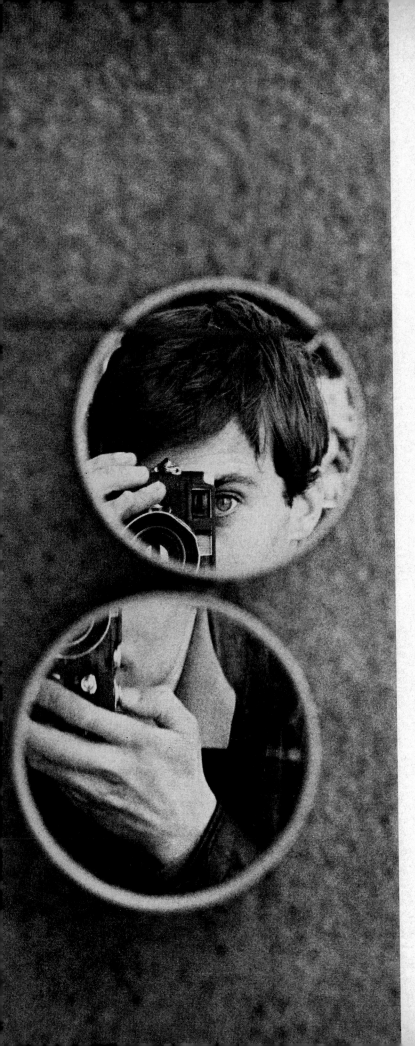

Those who follow the course of photography cannot help but notice the exciting and original work of Jeanloup Sieff. At only 32 he has already gained recognition as one of the leading contributors to this medium. Style and originality are the hallmarks of Sieff's photographs; his pictures are sensitive, yet powerful as you will see as you turn the pages of this portfolio.

Of Polish descent, Sieff was born in Paris in 1933. His interest in photography developed more or less as a hobby while he attended college. He had originally planned to be a movie director but abandoned this idea in favor of photography.

He then spent six months studying photographic techniques at an excellent school in Vevy, Switzerland and then returned to Paris where he began work as a free lance photographer. His capacity for discovering the essence of a photographic situation and analyzing it thoroughly is clearly expressed in his work. His creative ability, good taste and technical skills bring to his work an unusual variety of photographic possibilities. A few of which are displayed on these eight pages. The unusual self-portrait, to the left, was made because he saw a model's mirror hanging on the wall. Pages 107, 110 and 111 are fashion illustrations done on assignment for *Harper's Bazaar*. Turn to pages 108 and 109 for two commentaries on American sentimentality, both photos taken in the West. Two strong statements in composition, page 112, rehearsal time at the Newport Jazz Festival and page 113, scaffolding around the old New York Times building on 42nd Street and Broadway. These pictures, taken with a Leica, Bronica and Nikon, testify to Jeanloup Sieff's superb skill with the 35mm camera.

WILLIAM GELABERT

The interesting design created on the sidewalk after salt had been thrown upon it to melt the snow plus the appearance of a black cat resulted in this moody and dramatic picture taken by Gelabert during the day. He says: "Over printing made the cat appear to *float* and also emphasized the eyes." Born and raised in New York City, Gelabert took this photograph with a Leica M2 equipped with a Nikkor f/2.5 lens. The shutter speed was 1/60th of a second at an aperture of f/8. Exposure was on Plus-X film.

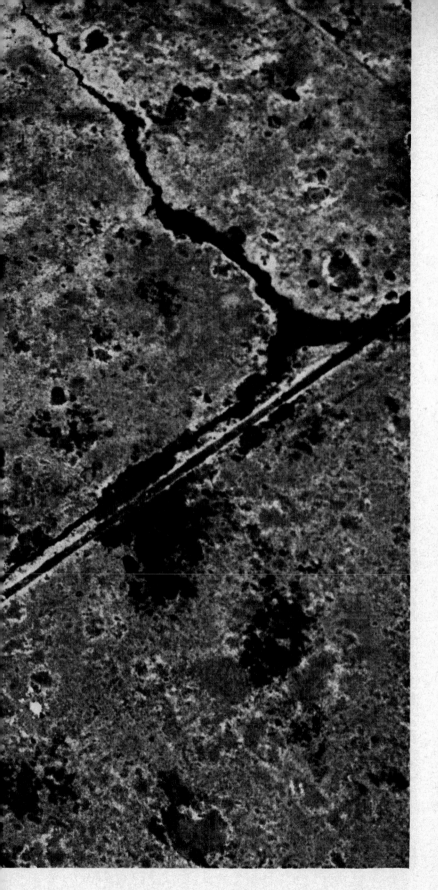

◄ **ROLF WINQUIST,** *Sweden (Page 114)*

One of the most accomplished and outstanding portrait and fashion photographers since 1930, Winquist's work has had wide acclaim both here and abroad. Tight framing increases the impact of the subject's casual expression in Winquist's head-on portrait of beautiful Birgitta Kembel. He used a Leica M3 with a 90mm lens. Exp. 1/250th of a sec. at f/5.6 on fast film. Diffused daylight.

◄ **ED LADA** *(Page 115)*

This nude study of a young lady hugging her body is not posed. Those goose pimples are the real thing. Lack of heat in Lada's studio caused him to ask the model if she would like to call the sitting off, being a good sport she said no. Lada, who has been photographing professionally for the past twelve years, took this picture with a Hasselblad, 150mm Sonnar lens. Speedlight bounced.

HORST TAPPÉ, *Germany*
(Pages 118 and 119) ►

Young German photographer, Horst Tappé, continues his portrait-taking parade of famous people from all walks of life. Two of his most recent acquisitions are Dali and Picasso. Dali was photographed in his dream house in Cadaques on the Costa Brava in Spain. Tappé met Picasso at a private showing of the painter's work in Antibes on the Cote D'Azur. Picasso graciously invited Tappé to photograph him in Cannes. Both of these strong and dynamic head shots were taken with a Hasselblad, Zeiss Sonnar 150mm lens. Exp. 1/60th of a sec. at f/8, Ilford HP3 film. Daylight.

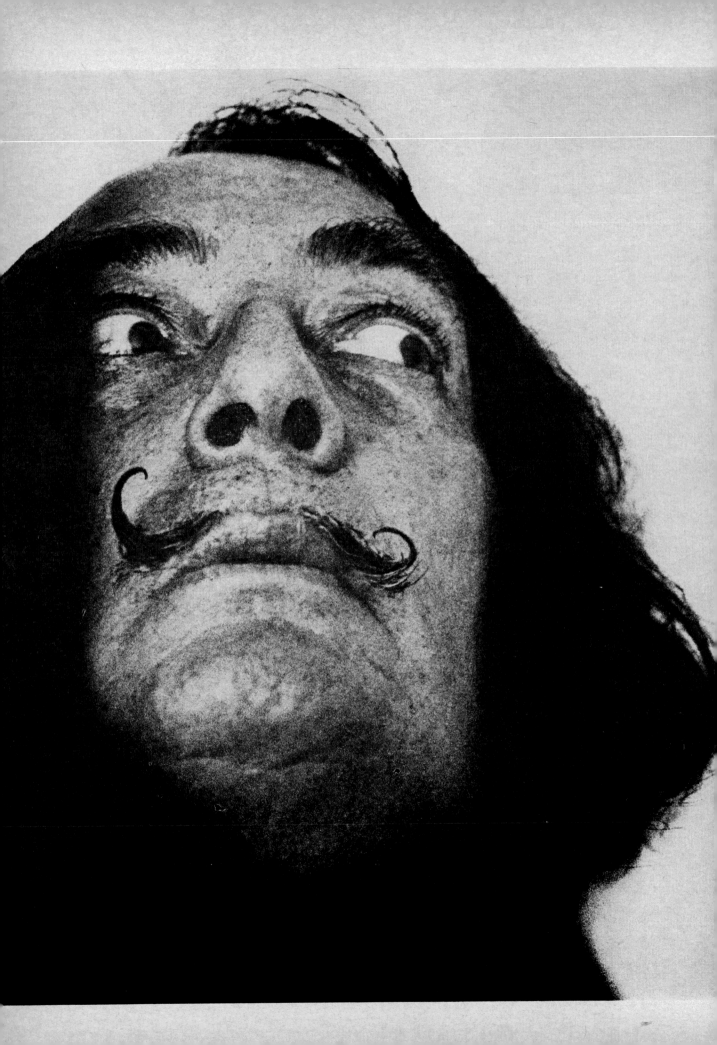

FOUR PAGES
ALL PHOTOGRAPHED
BY IRVING PENN

SCOTLAND

World-famous photographer, Irving Penn journeyed to Scotland a summer ago and spent about one month there on assignment for *Vogue* magazine. Three of his beautiful pictures of this dour and beautiful country follow on the next four pages.

Scotland lends itself to photography. It has soaring peaks and heather-clad moors, ancient castles and picturesque fishing villages. At all times of the year this is a land of color. Over all, so often, is that intense clarity of light which only an unsullied mountain land can give.

There is color and life, too, in the Highland Gatherings where tartan kilts swing to the skirl of the pipes; and in the festivals held in every center of Scotland during some time in the year.

This is the land of Bonnie Prince Charlie, Sir Walter Scott, Mary Queen of Scots and Robert Burns; where Highland chiefs held proud sway over their clans and fiery nobles warred for centuries.

Today the magic of Scotland with its scenic beauty and romantic appeal, its superstitions, fables and many legends continues to prevail.

Picture captions:

Opposite: Dewdrops on a thistle head, the flower of Scotland.

Pages 122-123: A seven-pound salmon, caught in the River Southesk, and photographed by natural light at ten in the evening.

Page 124: A street piper at Portobello, watched by a child just playing in the street.

A. BRUCE GOLDMAN

STEPHANIE DINKINS

HERBERT T. MARCUS *(Pages 128 and 129)* ▶

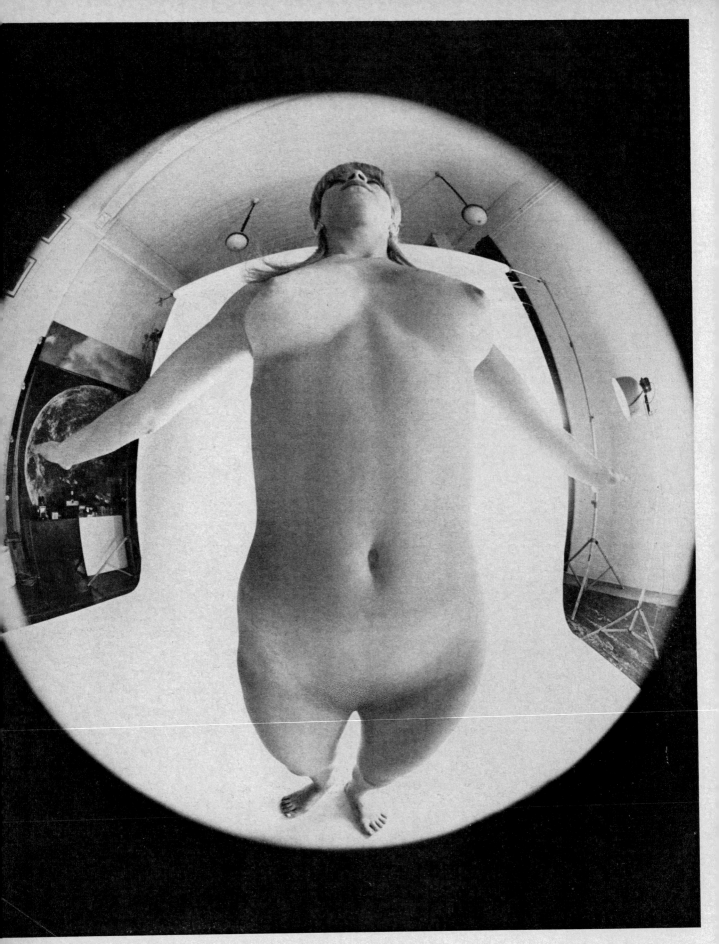

PHILIPPE HALSMAN *(Both pages)*

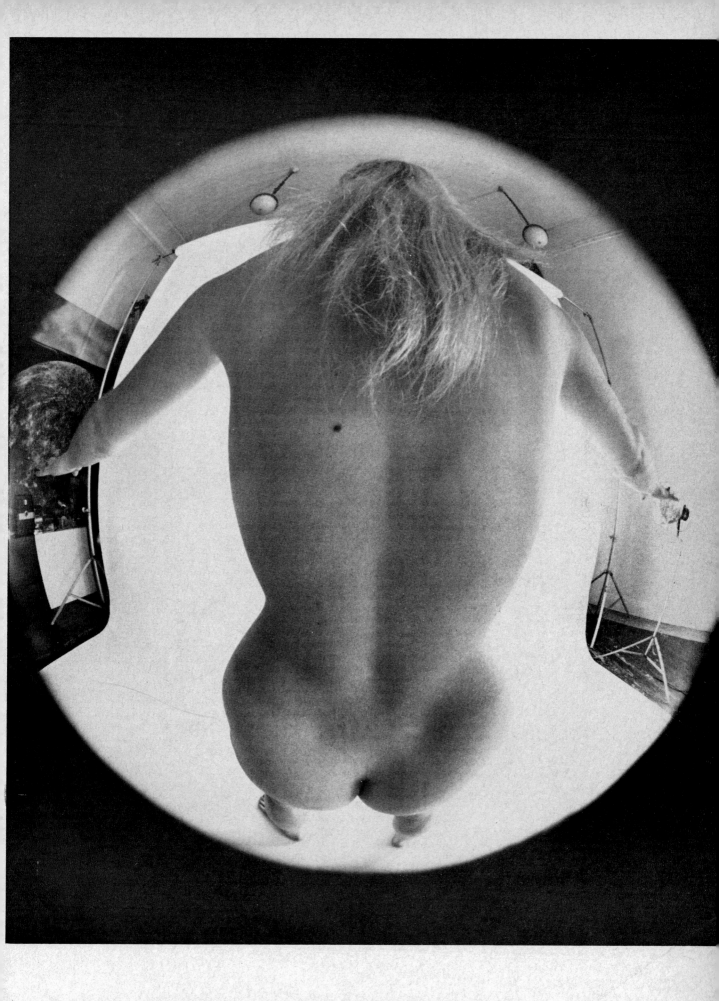

FRANCES McLAUGHLIN-GILL

JEAN PH. CHARBONNIER, *France* ▶

JAMES A. DRAKE, Jr.

For over a year James Drake has been taking pictures of the city of Philadelphia in preparation for a proposed book. The prints that appear across these two pages are a brief glimpse of what he says is, "an attempt to capture a mood—rather than compile the usual guidebook approach to a city." A native Philadelphian, Drake graduated from the University of Penn. He has been a magazine photographer for the past five years and his work has been seen in *Life*, *Saturday Evening Post* and *Sports Illustrated*, to name a few. Seven of these photos, taken between assignments, were made with a Leica M3. Three kids in museum, Nikon F.

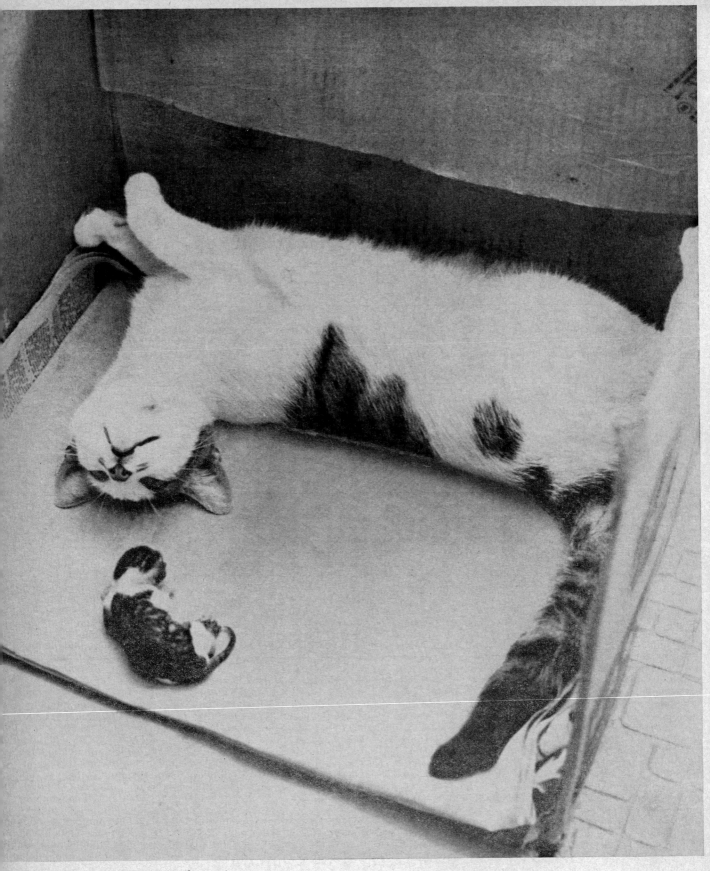

SUZANNE SZASZ *(Both pages)*

◀ BOB ROBINSON

(Pages 140 and 141)

In the autumn of 1963, Robinson did an essay on German refugees which appeared on the Norwegian State TV Services. This picture is from that series. Robinson, a native of California, went to Europe in 1952 and began free lancing for European publications. He has remained there since and is one of the original founders of the picture agency, Manité International, which is an organization dedicated to the practice of photo journalism. Nikon F. 1/60th at f/22 on Plus X film. Overcast day.

PATRICIA CAULFIELD

Pat Caulfield, who became interested in photography while in college at the University of Rochester, is an Executive Editor for *Modern Photography* magazine. She traveled to the now defunct Polo Grounds where she made this picture of the Met fans applauding a home run. Miss Caulfield's selective eye carefully framed the runner approaching the plate between the wildly waving arms of the Met spectators. She used a Leica M3 with a 35mm lens. The exposure was 1/125th of a second at f/11. Plus-X.

NORMAN LERNER *(Page 144)* ▶

Lerner has firmly established himself as a leading photographer in the fashion and advertising fields. "Figure photography," he says, "is basic for every photographer and should be explored as basic subject matter. It is one of the beauties and pleasures of life." Pentax camera with a 55mm lens. Speedlight.

JACK ANDERSSON *(Page 145)* ▶

This fine, carefully posed and composed picture was made by Andersson as an experimental study. He used a Hasselblad with an 80mm f/2.8 Tessar lens, exposed on Tri-X film. He used bounce flood to achieve the simple modeling and minimum of detail which add to this sculptural interpretation of the human body.

TERRENCE A. GILI *Pages (146 and 147)* ▶

While setting up his equipment to photograph two black Standard Schnauzers, one of them named Blitz took up a position and watched while he loaded his camera. Noting the near symmetry of his form, Gili quickly finished loading and set his lens, the result was this silhouetted portrait. The closeup photo of the crouching cat was taken while on assignment and appeared in the Yellow Pages, on subway and station posters and in national magazines. Gili, a most versatile photographer of animals, made both these pictures with a Mamiyaflex camera using Plus-X film and portable electronic flash.

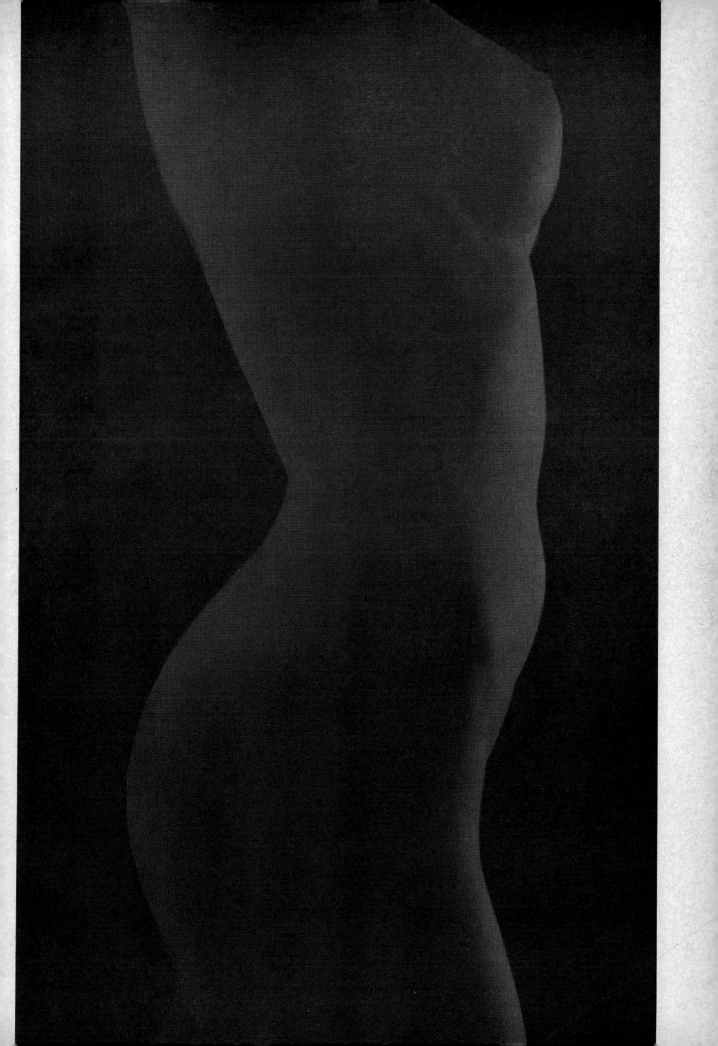

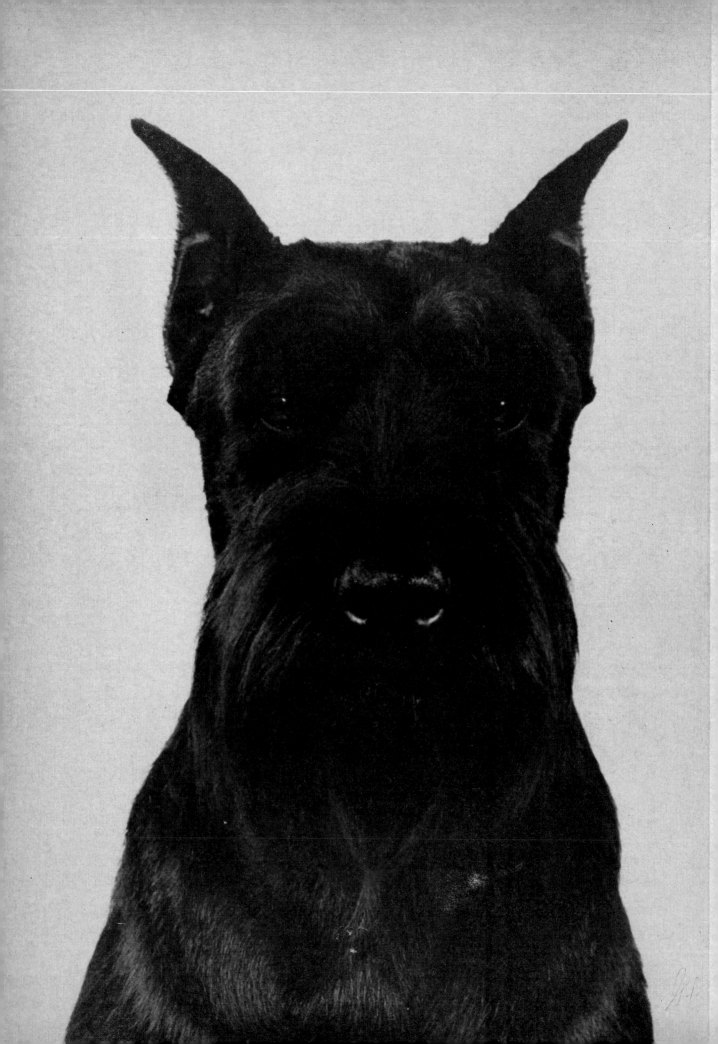

FRANK COWAN

FRANK Cowan is a precocious young man, but one feels that he is not aware of his precocity. Nor does he think it unusual that at the age of eighteen he firmly established himself in the minds of hard-hearted New York art directors when he walked in off the street with a portfolio of pictures, unsuited to their commercial needs, and was made welcome by instantaneous assignments.

Making good use of his multiple photographic talents, he was off to a flying start which has continued onwards and upwards over the past ten years.

Actually, he never had any dreams about becoming a great photographer and he can think of no valid reason that pointed him in that direction. At the request of his parents, he attended engineering school. This, he knew, was not the answer so after a year-and-a-half he left and, for want of something better to do, he turned to photography.

Art Director Art Cady of Young and Rubicam gave him his first agency job and with that assignment behind him he set up an experimental "studio" in his apartment. But most of his early work was done on location and in black and white only. He says, "I was really afraid of color and on top of that I didn't like it." Whatever fears he had vanished and he must of begun to like it, because 60% of Cowan's advertising illustrations are now shot in color. Just five years ago he opened up his own studio and the accounts started coming in fast and furious—and there has been no let up since.

He likes what he's doing, as he says, "It beats manufacturing shoes. However, I'd go crazy if I specialized in any one subject." A most versatile photographer, he is constantly searching for new techniques and new approaches to improve his work—one need never have fear of his going stale. At present he has a most competent staff including agent Nob Hovde, Bette Fleming, Casting Director and Stylist, Sture Lovquist, Studio Manager and Dan Ostrander, his assistant.

We began our conversation after introductions by Nob Hovde. He sat sprawled in a director's chair in a gentlemanly fashion and gazed at and fiddled with a construction ruler. It was then that I realized that he was not completely relaxed and he went on to say as much. However, as we talked back and forth and he ate and drank his way through a ham and swiss cheese sandwich and a chocolate malt, I found him to be a man of considerable intellectual range with a wry sense of humor (Continued on page 204)

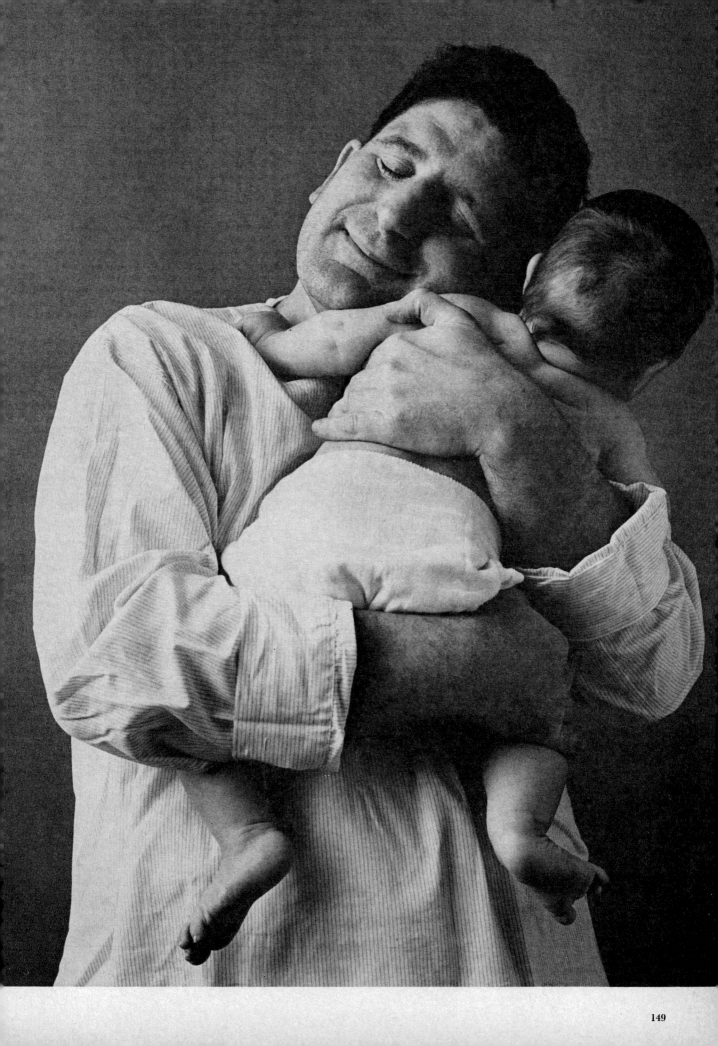

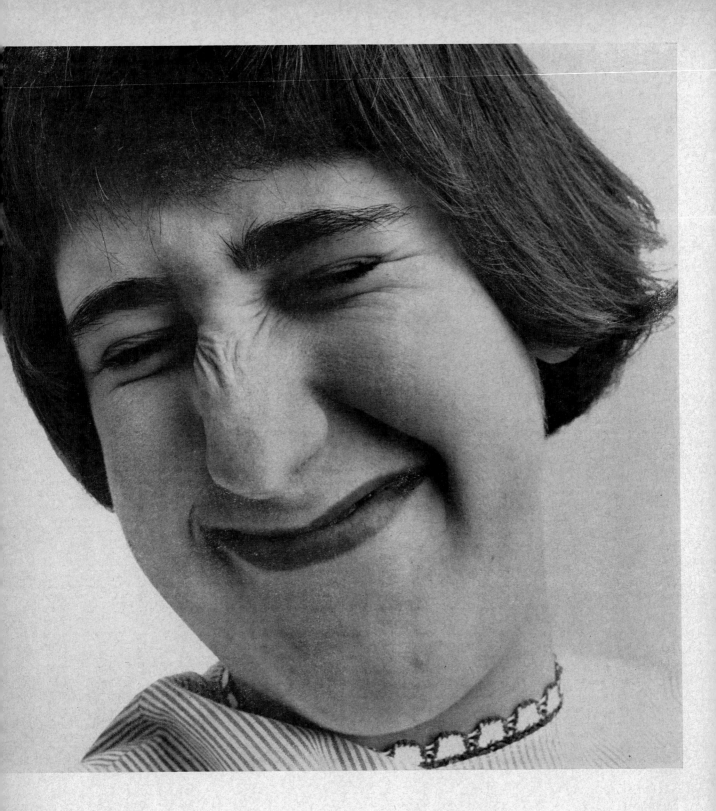

FRANK COWAN *(Both pages)*

FRANK COWAN *(Both pages)*

TODD WEBB (*Both pages*)

This door of a deserted house in the great old silver camp of Georgetown in the Colorado Rockies and the photograph of the grave in a Madrid, New Mexico cemetery high on a hill above the town, are both from a series taken by Webb to represent a portfolio of Western Ghost Towns. For over twenty-five years

Todd Webb has been known for his mastery of the camera. He used an 8x10 Deardorff with a 12 inch lens shooting at 1/10th of a sec. at f/4.5 on Super Pan Press film to make the photo of the door. For the grave, he used an Omega 120 with an f/3.5 lens. Exp. 1/100th of a second at f/16 on Plus-X film.

AD WINDIG, *Holland*

During a one minute silence commemorating the lib
eration of the Dutch from the Germans, Windig came
upon these four matrons during this most solemn occasion. Their pose and attitude (unintentional, of
course) gave the photo a satirical twist and Windig
says: "I'm glad to give *U.S. Camera* a contribution
which shows the more humorous side of my photography." He used a Rolleiflex with an Xenar f/3.5
lens. Exp. was 1/100 of a sec. at f/8. Ilford FP3 film.

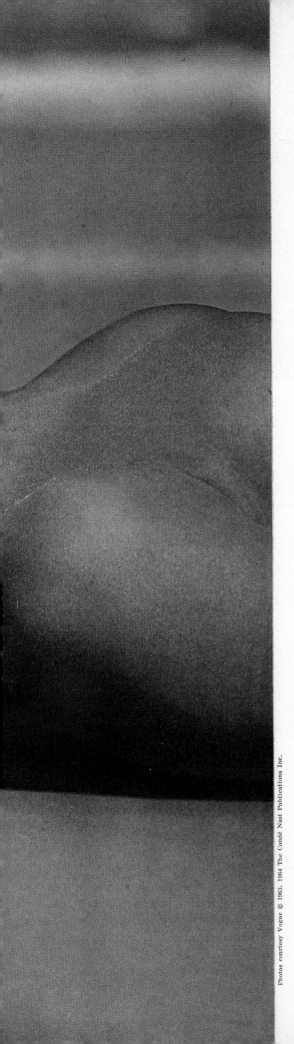

◄ **LEOMBRUNO-BODI** *(page 157)*

Sophia Loren. "In real life she has little in common with the fiery, hip-swinging Neapolitan peasant girl she often plays on the screen . . . . one notices her elegance . . . . wistfulness . . . . mystery, hinting at tragedy." From Francis Wyndham's interview for *Vogue* magazine, October 1, 1963 issue. Photographers Leombruno and Bodi took this picture, of one of the most beautiful and intriguing women in the world, on the movie set of *The Fall of the Roman Empire.*

HELMUT NEWTON *(and following page)*

Beauty on the beach. This exotic photograph taken by Mr. Newton on a beach in Australia, dazzles and excites the weakest of imaginations. On the following page, the sun-bronzed model wearing a kidskin bikini, was part of a special 32-page portfolio of racy new summer fashions all shot on location in Australia by Helmut Newton. Both pictures were done on assignment for, and recently appeared in, *Vogue.*

VITTORIO RONCONI, *Italy*

This portrayal of the figure is marked by the camera angle, pose and lighting. To emphasize the curves and flowing lines of the model's statuesque torso, Ronconi shot from a low angle. Ronconi, an insurance company employee, devotes all of his free time to his "hobby," photography and is a frequent contributor to magazines and journals both here and abroad. This fascinating study was made with a Rollei camera.

161

PETER FINK

Peter Fink has lived in and traveled around most of the world and much of this time has been spent photographing a great many places and people. Quiet and soft-spoken, he has quickly established himself among the top talent of the photography world.

Mr. Fink was at first an interior decorator by profession and made a name for himself by designing private houses as well as the salons of Lucien Lelong in Paris, Chicago, Los Angeles and New York. And, at one time, he was art director of Lanvin Parfums in New York. The transition to photography may not have been an easy one, but on the surface Peter Fink

seems to have made the jump with extraordinary ease. As a photographer, his impeccable instinct for design gives his photographs strong and visual impact.

At the moment, he is anxiously awaiting the publication of a book on New York City in which his pictures, both black and white and color, appear exclusively. It was an extremely exciting challenge of which he says, "It was a hell of an assignment to do the book since I had never done anything like that in this country and I really learned what New York was like." The photographs on these four pages will be part of the illustrations to appear in the

book. Architecture in New York may come and go but the Brooklyn Bridge goes on forever. It is pictured on page 162. The picture above could very well wind up being a collector's item for shortly after it was taken, this interior of Pennsylvania Station was demolished. Good composition must be functional and it is important to be able to select the arrangement of your picture elements to give the viewer a clear and effective idea of what your photograph is all about. These two buildings on pages 164 and 165 are perfect examples of Mr. Fink's control in composing a picture. His use of the strong directional lines of the buildings give off an exciting feeling of shapes and forms which help to produce a compelling compositional effect.

Peter Fink's work has been exhibited in such important museums as the Santa Barbara Museum of Art; the Seattle Art Museum; the Philbrook Art Centre in Tulsa; the Institute of Contemporary Art, Boston, the Biennale Institute, Grand Palais, Paris and the USIS Gallery, American Embassy in London. We could not reach him before he left for Europe on another assignment—so the only technical information available was the name of the camera—Rolleiflex.

PETER FINK

ANGELO LOMEO

JOSEF TICHY, *Czechoslovakia*

JAMES DRAKE

On January 29th of this year, the Winter Olympics began in the huge natural amphitheater around Innsbruck in Austria. More than 1,000 young athletes competed for the coveted medals that denote the peak of winter sports achievement. Spread across these two pages are quick glimpses of both contestant and spectator alike caught up in the kind of excitement that only an Olympics can produce. All the photographs were taken with a 35mm camera. James Drake, the photographer, is a young Philadelphian, who concentrates solely on editorial photography. These pictures, for instance, were taken on assignment for *Sports Illustrated*.

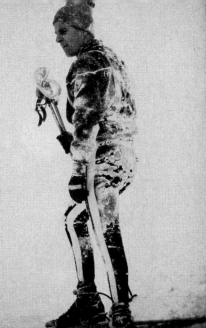

NAZARÉ

Photography by

KEN HEYMAN

Ken Heyman's enthusiasm for the village of Nazaré is briefly but convincingly expressed on these six pages. He was only able to spend seven shooting hours there, but in that short time, he came away full of cheers for this honest and lovely fishing village and was hungry for more. Needless to say, he will return shortly.

Portugal is not all petticoats and pictures but both are fairly high on the scale of Portuguese living.

So is Nazaré. Ken Heyman's portraits of Nazaré and its people follows, by a good number of years, Eliot Elisofon's Nazaré and its nets.

Upon his return from Europe, Heyman had these comments to make concerning Nazaré:

"I had just completed an exhaustive trip

that had taken me to thirteen countries (including India, Egypt and Sweden) and I was creatively spent. My last stop was Portugal before returning home to New York. I soon found myself in Nazaré, a small fishing village and resort town about three hours from Lisbon on the Atlantic coast.

"I consider myself a seasoned traveler (having photographed in more than 42 countries), but this village was fantastic. I believe it to be the most photogenic place I've ever seen. So much so that I intend to return in the next two years to spend several months photograph-

ing there. The whole set of photographs were taken with two cameras: an Asahi Pentax fitted with a 180mm Zeiss Sonnar lens and a Leica M2 with its 35mm Sumicron; Plus X film and a Lunasix light meter.

"I realized the photographic potential of the place within minutes after my arrival and only managed to steal a total of seven hours in my stay in Portugal to do my present set of pictures. The first photograph (pages 170 and 171) was taken from a great cliff overlooking Nazaré. While I was taking a view of the village, this old woman simply came over

and watched me—without saying a word. I backed off and put her in the right juxtaposition of the crashing waves far below.

"Nazaré was cold on the 29th of March (this year) when I was there, and the marvelous townswomen bundled themselves in their great black shawls. I like to think that the story I heard is true—that they come down from their homes to the shore to wait for their fishermen husbands. They would sit and wait stoically or gossip with their neighbors. They formed marvelous designs against the white sand and wouldn't bother to move if they happened to see the photographer pointing the camera in their direction.

"Just writing about Nazaré makes me want to return all the sooner."

We have a house in Portugal and my wife and I try to get there as often as we can. The house is in Arrabida, a Portuguese name as famous as Nazaré. Brett Weston's photo, pages 42-43, is of the view from our terrace overlooking the Atlantic ocean to the left and towards the ancient ruins of the Roman village of Troia on the right. We echo Ken Heyman's sentiments about Nazaré.   *Tom Maloney*

AN END –
AND A BEGINNING[*]

LOS ANGELES Coliseum in 1960. The late Pres. John F. Kennedy and Lyndon B. Johnson run on the Democratic ticket. While they fought each other for the presidential nomination, Johnson became an indispensable Kennedy vote-getter.

BILL BRIDGES

President Kennedy spent his last days engaged in the pursuit of re-election. Most of his time and energy would be devoted to two Southern states, they were Florida, with its 14 electoral votes and Texas, with 25, and it was to these that he went on his final journeys.

Now on a bright sunny morning in the city of Dallas, Texas he and Jackie were greeted at the airport by nearly 5,000 people and were welcomed by a committee who gave Mrs. Kennedy a bouquet of red roses. Then the cavalcade started into town. It had just passed through friendly crowds in the downtown section of Dallas and made a sharp left turn at the corner of Elm and Houston Streets, where the road heads down an incline toward an underpass. The Kennedys were smiling and waving as their car passed the Texas School Book Depository, then from the window of the sixth floor, Lee Harvey Oswald aimed his rifle and fired three times. In one swift, shattering moment, John Fitzgerald Kennedy, the youngest ever elected President, was dead. It was 12:30 p.m. C.S.T., blood gushed from the President's head as it came to rest in Jackie's lap. "Jack!" she cried. "Oh, no! No!"

Next to the initial shock and sorrow, the President's death touched off more worldwide grief and concern than anyone knew existed and Americans were confronted with the thought that they had in John F. Kennedy a more remarkable President than they had understood.

Just eighteen days before he was killed, Mr. Kennedy himself infused the day with a meaning that grew larger with his death. Finding much to be thankful in the American past, he counseled Americans to look to the future and to apply themselves anew to its fulfillment. "Let us earnestly and humbly pray," President Kennedy wrote, "that He will continue to guide and sustain us in the great unfinished tasks of achieving peace, justice, and understanding among all men and nations . . ."

Lyndon Baines Johnson, as one of his first official acts as President, directed that those words go forth to the nation on Thanksgiving eve. And soon after he personally went before a joint session of Congress to pledge himself to the unfinished tasks the late President had marked out—the tasks of peace, prosperity, and equality for all Americans. Thus with a certainty that reassured the U.S. and the world, President Johnson moved in quickly to take charge and all Americans silently joined him in that task.

CONVENTION TRI-UMPH. The primary road was rough and rugged and the clincher was the one in West Va. Kennedy won on the first ballot and then selected Lyndon Johnson to run for V.P. Kennedy was an avid sports fan and touch football was a family favorite. During his Senate days, he is seen above with his brother Bobby, Ted Sorenson and an unidentified friend.

OLLIE ATKINS

"Just as I went into politics because Joe died,
if anything happened to me tomorrow, my brother Bobby would run
for my seat in the Senate. And if Bobby died,
Teddy would take over for him."

TO ELEANOR HARRIS, 1957

A HAPPY TIME, Mr. and Mrs. John Fitzgerald Kennedy photographed at the time the announcement was made that he would actively seek the Democratic nomination. He then passionately sought the presidency and won. In the photograph directly above, his charm and way with people is captured during one of his many trips around the country; everywhere he went, well wishers sought to shake his hand or touch him. Such was the magic and popularity of this handsome young man who was cut down by an assassin's bullet in his 46th year. At right, the camera records another image of the late President, seen here in a reflective mood at a Senate Committee hearing in 1960.

"One of the issues of this campaign is my religion. I don't think it's
anyone's business but my business . . . Is anyone going to tell me that
I lost this primary 42 years ago on the day I was baptized?"

WEST VIRGINIA, 1960

181

"We have no wish to war with the Soviet Union, for we are a peaceful people who desire to live in peace with all other peoples. . . . The cost of freedom is always high, but Americans have always paid it. And one path we shall never choose, and that is the path of surrender, or submission."

COMMENCEMENT ADDRESS, AMERICAN UNIVERSITY, 1963

OLLIE ATKINS

ALONE AT work in his office, President John F. Kennedy sits at his desk doing his job. Always ready to answer any phone for whatever challenge it might bring. On the opposite page, the late President relaxes in his familiar rocking chair and gives his full attention to one of the many dignitaries who visited the United States throughout the year.

"And so, my fellow Americans: ask not what your country can do for you—ask what you can do for your country"

FROM INAUGURAL ADDRESS, 1961

"I will do my best. That is all I can do. I ask for your help—and God's

ANDREWS AIR FORCE BASE. 1963

LBJ Overcome with grief, Lyndon B. Johnson, standing aboard the President's Air Force jet, recited the thirty-four word oath of office and thus became the thirty-sixth President of the United States. Like the nation he now led,

1937 WITH ROOSEVELT. Johnson was appointed by F.D.R. to his first government post in National Youth Administration and helped him win in his first campaign.

1960 WITH TRUMAN. Johnson on way to lunch with old friend ex-President Truman. Under Truman, Johnson had been majority whip even though he was a freshman senator.

AS SHOCK AND disbelief at this dastardly act reverberated around the world, Lyndon Baines Johnson was sworn in as the 36th President of the United States. Pictured aboard the cramped compartment of the presidential plane, Air Force One, the new First Lady and the widowed one watched and listened in the privacy of their thoughts.

1957 WITH EISENHOWER. As a leader of a Democratic Congress under a Republican, Lyndon B. Johnson pushed Ike programs such as NATO, foreign aid.

WITH DOUGLAS-HOME

WITH DE GAULLE

WITH ERHARD

PRESIDENT JOHNSON AT HIS DESK

"The strong can be just in the use of strength"

WITH MIKOYAN

shocked and anguished in their mourning, life had to go on. And so, President Johnson moved in swiftly to take charge.

President Johnson had worked with four previous Presidents and during the time it took to take him from Texas to the White House he grew from a bright and agile young congressman to one of the most skillful, subtle and effective legislators our country has ever known. President Franklin D. Roosevelt was the first to discover Johnson and appointed him to his first government post in National Youth Administration and also helped him win his first campaign. Johnson was in the House for twelve years and was its first member to go to World War II. In 1948 he was elected Senator and then in 1953 he became minority leader in a Republican Senate. When the Dem-

L.B.J. ON ROCKER

WITH EDWARD STEICHEN AND CARL SANDBURG
WITH DEFENSE SECRETARY ROBERT McNAMARA

The father of a Queen

A PROUD FATHER, Johnson plants a kiss on the dimpled cheek of daughter Lynda Bird. The occasion was the Azalea Festival at Norfolk, Va. in 1961. Lynda Bird, then 17, was a most Gracious Queen.

ocrats took over the Senate he became majority leader under an opposite-party President and President Eisenhower called him "the best Democrat in the Senate."

As Kennedy's choice for Vice President, Mr. Johnson worked hard and long in the service of the administration. During this relationship, Lyndon Baines Johnson gained some insight into the size of his task. Once, after leaving Mr. Kennedy's office, he said: "The President carries heavier burdens than I ever envisioned. You feel little goose pimples coming up on your back because it's such a frightening, terrifying responsibility."

It now lies with him.

GATHERED AT the fence of their 400-acre ranch are Lyndon B., Luci Baines, Lynda Bird and Lady Bird. Most of their hunting dogs also have names with LBJ initials. This photograph was made before Johnson became the 37th Pres. of the U.S.

Photographic Data

66   RENÉ JACQUES, *France*

Noting the reflection of the Place Vendôme in a Christmas ornament, Jacques set up his camera on a tripod and proceeded to make this unusually clear picture of the famous street. Shooting from inside his studio, he used a Linhof camera with a Super Angulon Schneider lens. The exposure was ½ second at an aperture of f/32. Daylight, Ilford film.

67   PHILIPP GIEGEL, *Switzerland*

Giegel made this picture at one of the performances of the show, *Holidays On Ice*, in Zurich in 1963. To get the blurred effect, he shot at a comparatively low speed, 1/15th of a second at f/8, while horizontally following the movement of the skating couple. Swiss-born Giegel, who has three distinguished books on early Christianity to his credit, used a Hasselblad 500C with a 250mm lens. Spotlights, Tri X film.

73   DAN YOUNG

A native of Arizona, Young attended the Art Center School. He has been photographing in Europe since 1962 and his work is constantly appearing in both European and American publications. He is a member of Manité International, an organization founded in Oslo, Norway in 1962 by a group of people seeking to establish a central organization through which they could develop their individual aims and yet strengthen their position by acquiring organizational status in the field. Young says of this fashion shot: "Assignment called for bizarre handling without destroying the line of the clothing. Hellen, the Norwegian model, added greatly to the success of the picture." Nikon F with a 28mm lens. Exp. 1/150th of a second at f/16, slightly overcast sun. Plus X.

98   MICHAEL PEIRCE

The mobility of movement primarily belongs to kids. And, Michael Peirce took advantage of this characteristic when his son climbed up onto a chair in the living room and made this charming photograph in which the child and the chair seem to be made for each other. An advertising photographer, who resides in Cambridge, Mass., Peirce used a Mamiyaflex camera, 80mm lens. 1/125 at f/8. Speedlight, Plus X film.

99   ATHANASIOS TSAGRIS, *Greece*

While on a touring trip to Olympia, Tsagris passed through the small village of Tropea where he paused and took this photograph of an older sister holding her younger brother. The tender way in which she held him and the expressions on their faces greatly influenced Tsagris. He used a Rollei with a 75mm lens. 1/60th of a sec. at f/5.6. Born in Peloponese, Greece, 1926, Tsagris has been a free lance photographer since 1950 and specializes in photojournalism.

100   RENÉ-JACQUES, *France*

One of the most traveled roads in the world leads to the famous cathedral in the city of Chartres. The illusion of depth is made possible by the natural arrangement of the road, trees, and the church off in the distance. A well-known professional photographer, Jacques made this picture with a Graphic camera, 127mm lens. The shutter speed was 1/100th of a second at f/16. He exposed on Double X film.

101   TODD WALKER

This photograph of a street in San Francisco was taken by Walker in conjunction with an assignment. To him, the picture captured a different essence of this city, which he feels is usually photographed in postcard fashion. This arresting study in pattern composition was made with an Asahi Pentax camera, using a 250mm Sonnar lens. He exposed on Tri X film at 1/100th of a second at an aperture of f/5.6.

102   SHOSUKE YAMAGUCHI, *Japan*

Mr. Yamaguchi has been an amateur photographer since 1958, his favorite subject is animals. To get this picture, Yamaguchi patiently waited long hours while six sea lions playfully swam about. Finally, the largest one floated up to the surface and looked Yamaguchi straight in the face; the humorous expression and the pattern the water made dripping from the sea lion's head was what he had been waiting for. Born in Osaka City, Japan in 1898, Mr. Yamaguchi used a Leica M3 with a Hektor 135mm lens. He exposed at 1/250th of a second at f/11. Natural light.

103   ALFRED GESCHEIDT

"This," says Gescheidt, "is almost a full frame—which shows how close you can come with the standard 50mm lens." This comical closeup of a neighbor's son closely examining a frog he caught in Gescheidt's pond, was taken with a Pentax at 1/500 at f/5.6.

104-105   HASSE HANSON, *Sweden*

Hasse Hanson carefully arranged the bottles in the

On Fine Pictures

picture on page 104 and just as carefully placed the different objects that appear on page 105. The result affords the viewer an opportunity to look at two strong compositions in still life studies. A professional, Hanson specializes in advertising and industrial photography. He took both these photographs with a Hasselblad 500C camera with a 150mm lens. For the bottles he exposed at 1/15th of a second at f/8. For the wheelbarrow, etc., ¼th of a second at f/16. Both Panatomic film, both on a cloudy day.

125 RONALD E. REIS

This photograph was taken at a Greenwich Village outdoor art show. Of it Reis says, "This woman was one of the exhibitors. She was amused by the fact that I was taking her picture, just as I was by the picture she presented." Reis, a partner in a neckwear manufacturing firm, has made photography his hobby for the past three years and has been most successful in both fields. He used a Leica M3, 135mm lens.

128-129 HERBERT T. MARCUS

Herbert Marcus, whose brilliant circus trapeze pictures were featured in a portfolio of the 1964 edition of *U.S. Camera Annual*, has this to say: "This shot is part of a series of the elegant and daring performer, billed as Princess Tajana. The exposure for this series was quite tricky because the number of spotlights and their color changed every few seconds. The whole series was shot at 1/250 with an aperture range from f/2.8 to 18 (guess and keep your fingers crossed technique). It works. The specks are 'soap bubbles' that are not made of soap. I don't know what the compound is." Nikon SP.

126 A. BRUCE GOLDMAN

The New York World's Fair has been and will continue to be the target of cameras until the day it closes. But, we think this picture is the most interesting and unusual one that we've come across. Goldman admits he was rather cynical about the Fair and he set out to take a picture that would reflect his attitude. The dinosaur proved to be the perfect foil, for with it, Goldman created a science fiction-like quality in which the animal completely overpowered the Fair. Professional photographer Goldman used a Rolleiflex with a 75mm lens. Exposure was 1/125th of a second at f/8. Plus X film, available light.

127 STEPHANIE DINKINS

Outside of Rome, Miss Dinkins took this picture of the Canopus Pool of Hadrian's Villa while doing a picture story about new archaeological discoveries unearthed there. The brooding rain storm in the distance greatly added to the mood of the photo. Miss Dinkins has been photographing since 1957 and in that short time, she has illustrated three books and her work has been published in magazines of note both here and abroad. Rolleiflex with a 75mm lens. Shutter speed, 1/125th of a second on Plus X film.

130-131 PHILIPPE HALSMAN

The young lady pictured on these two pages could very well be someone from Mars. However, she's from this planet but has been made a victim (willing) of the fish eye lens. You can have a lot of fun with this lens because you get an extra-wide field of view—180 degrees. Then, the depth of field is almost unlimited. The photo is actually a 24mm-diameter circle on a 36x24mm negative. This means you can leave the circle for a rounded view, or crop right into it for an even more unusual effect. The distinguished photographer, Philippe Halsman, put aside his famous Fairchild-Halsman camera and used a Nikon. The aperture was f/11, speedlight, Tri X film.

132 FRANCES McLAUGHLIN-GILL

This expressive portrait of singer Miss Georgia Brown was made on assignment in London for *Vogue*. Frances McLaughlin-Gill, whose pictures appear "all over the place," feels that theatre people make rather marvelous subjects. They automatically "turn on," so accustomed are they to audiences. This photograph in which Miss Brown is singing along with one of her records, was taken with a Hasselblad with a 180mm lens. Exposure was 1/50th of a second at f/4.5. Lighting, direct single flood. Film, Tri X.

133 JEAN-PH. CHARBONNIER, *France*

This picture of U.S. Defense Secretary, Robert S. McNamara, is one of a series taken by Charbonnier while on assignment for his magazine, *Réalités*. During this sitting they spoke about their mutual interest in mountain climbing and skiing among other topics and Charbonnier remembers the meeting as one of the easiest VIP's he'd ever worked with. He used a Topcon camera with a 100mm lens. The exposure was 1/60th of a second at f/4. Artificial light. Tri X.

136 TOM JUNGMAN

The occasion for this photograph was Armed Forces

Photographic Data On Fine Pictures

Day, which took place on Governor's Island. Wandering around the grounds and listening to the band playing for the people, Jungman caught their reflection in this musician's instrument. Jungman felt it was a good graphic description of the event. He used a Nikon F camera with a 58mm lens for this shot. He exposed at 1/250th of a second at f/16 on Tri X film.

137   CARL FRANK

Free lance photographer Carl Frank spent eight months traveling across the continent of Africa during which time he covered over 15 countries—from the Cape to Cairo. It was in the Wankie Reserve in Southern Rhodesia that he shot this picture of a bull elephant. A distance of 20 ft. separated the charging elephant and the moving car—using a Canonflex with an 85mm lens, Frank filled up the entire 35mm frame adding to the enormity of the animal's size.

138-139   SUZANNE SZASZ

Last September was the publication date of *The Silent Miaow*, a wonderful book about a cat called Cica. The photos that appear on these two pages are from it. Suzanne Szasz has this to say about them. "These are part of 300 photographs I made on the life of my cat—from the moment she appeared at the door as a lost kitten, to her growing up and our taking care of her as our own. There is nothing a working photographer needs more than to live with a fascinating, new, challenging subject. I can't remember when it gave me so much pleasure to photograph. I had never had a cat or kitten before, so there were new discoveries every day. More than 200 of the pictures are in this book." It's a beautiful book for people who love animals. Miss Szasz, who is an expert on child photography, used a Rollei.

166   ANGELO LOMEO

To emphasize the imposing size of the columns of St. Peter's Square, Lomeo waited for a long time for the right human figure to appear and by its smallness give depth to the photograph. The nun also brings to the picture a significant religious connotation. Lomeo, a free lance photographer, used a Nikon F with a 50mm lens. 1/60 of a sec. at f/16. Plus X.

167   JOSEF TICHY, *Czechoslovakia*

Tichy's selective eye enabled him to see the essence of composition in this picture of the continuing staircase. He chose the right angle and while the people flowed up and down the stairs, he made his move and obtained the effect he wanted. Born in 1914 and a successful photographer for some time, Tichy made this photograph with a Rolleiflex, 75mm lens. The exposure was 1/30th of a second at f/5.6.

34-35   HANS W. SILVESTER, *West Germany*

In 1858 an apparition of the Virgin Mary was said to have been seen in Lourdes, a town in Hautes-Pyrénées, France. It has remained to this day, a scene of remarkable cures. Moved by the unending arrivals of the faithful, tended to by volunteers from all over the world, Silvester made this appealing photograph. Born in Germany, Silvester has been residing in a little village in Provence, France. His most recent work was his book, *Frankreich*, published last August. To make this picture, he used a Leica M2.

37   MATTHEW E. HARLIB

Of these two photographs Harlib says: "These are part of a series of photographs exploring line and pattern of nature in terms of 'pure' black and white. Exercises in selectivity and isolation, through photographic means of forms, rhythms and patterns with emotional content. Negatives exposed, developed and printed for high contrast—all texture subdued." Television producer and director Harlib used a 35mm camera, 50mm lens on a dull grey day.

42-43   BRETT WESTON

This magnificent view can be seen in its original splendor as you approach the still undiscovered town of Portino de Arribida in Portugal. Brett Weston photographed this breath-taking sight with an 8x10 Ansco View camera with a 12" Tessar lens. He exposed at 1/5th of a second at f/32. Versapan film.

44-45   KORO HONJO, *Japan*

Koro Honjo is a man who is enchanted by the beauty of the female figure. Experimentation with the varying shapes of the human body provided Honjo with these two provocative and unusual female forms. Honjo, who manages a photo studio in Nishinomiya near Kobe, made the two photographs with a Minolta camera, artificial light, exposed on Neopan SS film.

You'll never miss another picture because it's raining or snowing or hailing, or because it's too damp, too dry, too cold, too warm...or too anything!

This new, amphibious all-weather '35' by Nikon even takes pictures under water without a housing.

The new Nikonos is a camera you can have with you where you'd ever risk using another. Hermetically sealed, salt water resistant, fungus- and mildew-proof, is virtually indestructable.

Grime, mud, sand, dust — they have no effect on the Nikonos. You simply rinse it under the tap, and it's as good as new.

It can weather the worst the elements can offer, water pressure to 160 feet below the surface, even exposure to radioactive dust.

What makes the Nikonos so extra-special is that it is a great fair-weather camera, too — trim, compact — fast and easy to handle. Uses standard color and black & white 35mm film; accepts flash,

filters and other accessories; and it is equipped with a fabulous 35mm Nikkor f2.5 lens — removable and interchangeable. Price is only $169.50.

For complete details, write to Department US-65.
Nikon Incorporated
111 Fifth Ave. New York 3, N. Y.
Subsidiary of Ehrenreich Photo-Optical Industries, Inc. In Canada: Anglophoto Ltd., Montreal 9, P. Q.

See the Nikon exhibit at the World's Fair — Japan Pavilion

195

"ABSOLUTELY THE BEST BEGINNER'S PHOTO BOOK..."
James Hughes, *Industrial Photography*

EVERYBODY'S PHOTO COURSE

ABOUT THE BOOK

Everybody's Photo Course contains 33 lessons in photography covering FUNDAMENTALS • EXPOSURE • DEVELOPING • ENLARGING • COMPOSITION • LIGHTING • ACTION • LENSES • FILTERS • FLASH • POSING • PORTRAITURE • PROPS • CLOSE-UPS and a great deal more including numerous shooting assignments planned to help you see, take and make better pictures. This large format (same size as this page) 144-page book contains more than 40,000 words of instructional text and over 750 illustrations. This is *the* book every amateur — beginner, novice or advanced photographer — needs. Get your copy now on newsstands, in book stores, camera stores or by mail from U.S. Camera.

Heavy Paperback edition $1.95
Deluxe laminated hardcover edition . $2.95

Here's what the critics say:

"More than 750 photographic illustrations are used by Joseph Foldes in his *Everybody's Photo Course* . . . to teach photography step by step in one of the most unusual and helpful beginner's books in the field . . . In thirty-three lessons of text and pictures, notable for their clarity and comprehensiveness, the author-teacher-photographer supplies the beginner with all the guidance he will need for a long time to teach himself photography".
Jacob Deschin, N.Y. Times

"It is written in the nature of self-assignments and here, the photographer studying it is in for some real self-discipline, which, of course, will pay off if he is diligent".
Alva L. Dorn, Kalamazoo Gazette

"It's a great book for the camera owner who wants to do better".
St. Petersburg Time

"What better way is there to teach photography than the use of the medium itself in the form of 750 illustrations. Learn by doing is the theme in the self-assignment picture taking exercises. The photographer can compare his results with the do and don't illustrations in the book".
John Reidy, N.Y. Daily Mirror

"This is not a book you read once and put aside. It is a 'how to do it' manual on photography and you will refer to it many times—especially when you have a problem. There are invaluable tips on posing, lighting and backgrounds that alone are worth the price".
Monte Ito, Honolulu Advertiser

"A once-over-lightly of this course convinces you it is factual, helpful, complete, understandable, workable and authentic. Anyone who absorbs the information contained therein will become a better photographer, that's certain".
Ralph Miller, N.Y. World Telegram & Sun

An unsolicited letter from a reader:

"I received my copy of *Everybody's Photo Course* in the deluxe laminated hardcover. I am a Pharmacist, and attempted in the brief span of time I have had it to evaluate how very, very valuable this book is to everyone concerned with photography. Mr. Foldes is a master at putting his subject over and the book is very, very well done.

"I am so enthused over the *Everybody's Photo Course* that I am enclosing my check in the sum of $5.85 for which please send me three copies of *Everybody's Photo Course* in the heavy paperback edition. I intend to make presents of these to friends of mine".
Alfred Trahan, New Orleans 19, La.

U.S. CAMERA PUBLISHING CORP.
9 EAST 40th ST., NEW YORK 16, N.Y.

Gentlemen:

I am enclosing my personal check ☐ money order ☐

in the amount of $.............. for .... copies of *Everybody's Photo Course* in heavy paperback edition at $1.95 each ☐; in deluxe laminated hardcover edition at $2.95 each ☐.

Name ....

Street ....

City.................... Zone....... State................

Get started with PROGRESS

GEORGE W. MARTIN

When you go, go FIRST CLASS. Whether you hop on your motorcycle or simply pick up a phone and dial, you can be confident that PROGRESS, specialists in engravings, will give you the professional touch your pictures demand. Years of experience in producing clean, accurate engravings has made PROGRESS a name to remember. A company whose skill and reputation is respected throughout the photo-engraving industry. Roar in at the finish line by being number one with PROGRESS.

Next time you think of engravings think of PROGRESS . . . call or write for one of our representatives

PROGRESS *Photo Engraving Company, Inc.*

12 JOURNAL SQUARE, JERSEY CITY, NEW JERSEY
OLDFIELD 3-0717-0718

U.S. CAMERA SUGGESTS . . .

Color Photography, *by Elisofon* **$10.00**
A "must" for your photographic library.

How to Sell Your Pictures at a Profit
$1.95
New Edition of Photographers' Market
Place.

Everybody's Photo Course
by Foldes ppr., **$1.95;** hard, **$2.95**

How To Process Color Film At Home
$2.50
Practically fool-proof step-by-step procedures
for the amateur.

Successful Freelance Photojournalism,
by McIntosh **$6.50**
Theory and practice of photojournalism. 128 pp.

Practical Way to Perfect
Enlargements *by Foldes* **$5.00**

Fred Archer on Portraiture **$5.75**
The best in the field.

Technique of Film Editing
by Reisz **$9.95**
Practical solutions to film making problems.

Filming in Colour
by D. Townsend **$2.95**
A real guide for those who shoot in colour.

Posing Patterns
by L. E. Broome **$10.00**
650 female photographic poses with variations in diagrammatic form.

Amateur Photographer's Handbook
$5.95

Technique Of The Sound Studio
Nisbett **$10.50**
Describes in detail all procedures necessary to
record sound.

Technique Of Film & Television
Make-Up, *Kehoe* **$9.00**
Covers the whole subject with thorough treat-
ment on the methods of make-up, both black
& white & color.

Technique of Film Animation
by Hales and Manvell **$10.00**
The first complete handbook on all aspects
of animation.

American Cinematographer Manual
A.S.C. **$7.50**
The 'bible' of Hollywood cameramen.

Total Picture Control
by Feininger **$7.50**
Gives complete control over every element in
every conceivable kind of situation.

Better Color Movies
by Fred Bond **$4.95**
An authority on 8mm & 16mm color movies.
Day & night-time movie making.

Advertising Photography
by Pinney **$12.50**
The significant role of photography in visual
selling.

POLAROID MANUAL
by Adams **$5.95**
The only Polaroid Technical Handbook.
192 pages, with 32 prints by professionals.

West Virginia in Color **$4.00**
The beauty of West Virginia only told in color.

Coloring, Tinting & Toning
by Walley **$3.95**
Instructions and methods for obtaining col-
ored effects.

Manual of Sound Recording **$13.95**
Elementary and highly specialized on sound
recording. All phases.

Graphic Graflex Photography
by Morgan **$6.95**
How to make prize-calibre pictures.

Make Your Own Color Prints
by Bagby **$4.50**
How to make fine color prints with new color
negatives and Ektacolor paper.

How To Use Your Camera Underwater,
by H. Dobbs **$6.50**
Underwater houseings, films, cameras, special
lighting, skin diving, etc.

Manual Of Applied Photography
$19.95
3000 hints and tips on the uses of photography.

German Photographic Annual
$10.00
German camera craftsmanship.

Technique of Bird Photography
by Warham **$5.95**
An excellent training manual and reference
work.

Strobe—The Lively Light
by H. Luray **$5.95**
The only complete and authoritative book on
electronic flash. For black/white and color.
120 illus.

Photo Lab Index, *by Carroll* **$25.00**
The only Encyclopedia of its kind.
The largest single collection of photograph-
ic data.

Leica Manual & Data Book **$6.95**
Practical information on 35mm photography.

Posing for the Camera
by Shepard & Meyer **$6.95**
A Professional Guide for the creative Model.

Close Up Photography With Your
Camera, *by Martin* **$2.50**
Covering microphotography and photomicro-
gaphy.

The Exakta Handbook
by Allison **$2.95**
How to understand your camera.

How to Retouch and Spot Negatives
and Prints, *by Floyd* **$2.50**
Professional techniques and how to use them.

Complete Book Of Nature
Photography, *by Russ Kinne* **$7.50**
A "must" for the working naturalist.

Pocket Photo Data Book,
Morgan & Morgan. In Vinyl **$3.95**
Covers film speed, guide numbers, etc.

How to Tell a Living Story with Home
Slides, *by Kinney* **$3.95**

The World Through My Eyes
by Andreas Feininger **$12.50**
The finest achievements of a LIFE magazine
photographer.

Cats, *by M. Adam* **$4.95**
For cat lovers. 10 color and 99 monochrome
illustrations.

Medical Photography in Practice
by Linnsen **$15.00**
A source book for all engaged in all branches
of medical photography.

The Nude, *by Andre DeDienes* **$4.95**
Another fabulous portfolio by a master.

Better Color Slides Indoors:
Better Color Slides Outdoors
by Bond
How to produce good color slides under all
conditions.
Each **$1.95**   Both **$3.50**

Cameras: The Facts **$7.95**
How They Work; What They Will do; and How
They Compare.

Principles Of Cinematography
by Wheeler **$13.95**
Present day motion picture production and
exhibition.

Science of Photography
by Baines **$7.9**
Evolution of photography and its modern application.

Art & Visual Perception
by Arnheim **$12.5**
Better composition through actual studies.

Exposure Manual, *by Dunn* **$9.9**
A comprehensive survey of exposure determ-
nation.

Making 8mm Movies
by Philip Grosset **$7.9**
Covers camera, screening, directing, etc.

Tape Recorder Manual
by Sharps **$5.9**
Technical information for all uses.

Better Colour With Walter Benser
$6.5
A guide to successful color photos.

Making & Printing Color Negatives
by Vickers **$6.9**
Complete course on use of color print ma
terials.

Special Effects in Cinematography
by Bulleid **$5.9**
Covers animation, super-imposition, optic
effects, etc.

A Child's Garden of Verses
by Stevenson **$2.9**
Completely revised.

Daybooks of Edward Weston:
Mexico I **$10.0**

Design in Motion
by Hala and Manvell **$12.5**
A most flourishing field of modern art.

Movie Techniques For The Advanced
Amateur, *by Regnier* **$4.9**
8mm & 16mm, from script to screen.

Delights Of Photography
by G. Reid **$5.9**
Every facet of photography is covered ar
illustrated by more than 170 photos.

Lenses In Photography
by R. Kingslake **$5.9**
Background of fundamental optical knowledg
for the photographer.

Designs by Photography
by Croy **$8.9**
The frontiers where photography and graph
design overlap. A wealth of unorthodox tech
niques. 174 pp. 425 illustrations.

Copying and Reproduction
by Croy **$8.9**
The technique of control in copying. 276 pp
74 illustrations.

Photographing People, *Wallace* **$2.9**
The author helps the reader to achieve perfe
results.

Cine Photography for Amateurs
by Wallace **$2.9**
For the newcomer to cine and for the prac
tised amateur.

Making Photography Pay
by Wallace **$2.9**
Advice on type of picture likely to appeal.

Choosing & Using a Cine Camera
by E. Gilmour **$2.9**
Guide to choosing a camera, various mecha
ical & optical features.

Exposing Cine Film, *B. Gibson* **$2.9**
Basic and advanced principles of exposur

Cine Titling *by J. Daborn* **$2.9**
New ideas in design, lettering and style;
well as novelties.

Lighting for Cine *by B. Gibson* **$2.9**
Natural and artificial lighting. Film, filter
exposures, etc.

Books You Shouldn't Be Without . . .

BEST SELLING GUIDES . . . . . $1.95 each

Agfa-Optima Guide, Tydings.
Amateur 8mm Movie Guide, Norinsky.
Amateur Photographer's Model, Stinger.
Animal Photography, Dunton.
Ansochrome & Ektachrome Home Processing.
Argus 35mm Guide, Tydings.
Art of Glamour Photography, Yeager.
Available Light Guide, Kinzer.
Available Light Photography, Latham.
Baby & Child Photog, Murphy.
Basic All 35mm Camera Shooting, Tydings.
Basic All 8mm Movie Shooting, Tydings.
Basic 8mm Movie Reference Guide, Pollack.
Basic Photography, Weisbord.
Beginner's Guide to Color Photography, Costa.
Bell & Howell Movie Guide, Tydings.
Beseler Enlarger Guide, Coles.
Better 8mm Home Movie Guide, Duitz.
Better Electric Eye Movies.
Better Photography for Amateurs, Fenten.
Binoculars & Scopes & Their Uses in Phg., Reichert.
Bolex Movie Guide, Tydings.
Bolex B8-C8 Guide.
Bounce Guide.
Camera Techniques for Color Movie Makers.
Candid Photography, Wahl.
Candid Wedding Photography.
Canon 35mm Camera Guide.
Close-up & Copying Photography, Simmons.
Color Printing, Engdhal.
Complete Lighting Guide.
Composition in Photography, Wagg.
Contaflex Guide, focal.
Creative Color, Rothstein.
Creative Figure Photography.
De Jur Movie Guide, Tydings.
Earning Money with Your Movie Camera.
Editing Your Own Color Movies.
Edixa Reflex Guide.
Exakta-Exa Guide, Emanuel & Rothschild.
Exakta-Exa Guide, Tydings.
Experimental & Trick Phg., Duckworth.
Exposure Meter Guide, Coles.
Electronic Flash, Gowland.
8-16mm Movie Eqpt. Rating Guide.
Family Photography, Kuhner.
Filter Guide, Latham.

Fujica Guide.
Getting Started in Photography, Barry.
Graphic & Linhof Press Camera Guide, Tydings.
Graphic 35mm Guide, Kingsbury.
Guide to Perfect Exposure.
Guide to Photographic Composition, Jonas.
Handbook of 35mm Camera Practice, Tydings.
Hand-Coloring Your Photographs, West.
Home Movies in Sound, Murphy.
Honeywell Pentax SRL Guide, Tydings.
How to Capture Action in Photog, Daniels.
Hunting with Camera & Binoculars, Sell.
Improved 35mm Techniques, Jones.
Instant Lens Testing Chart, Tydings.
Keystone Movie Guide, Tydings.
Kodak Brownie Star Cameras, Tydings.
Kodak 8mm Brownie Movie Camera, Tydings.
Kodak Miniature Camera Guide, Tydings.
Legal Aspects of Photography, Sherwin.
Leica Guide, Amphoto.
Lens Technique for Color Movie Magic.
Lighting in Photography, Simmons.
Making Slide Duplicates, Rothschild.
Mamiya C Series Twin Lens Reflex, Tydings.
Mamiya-16 Camera Guide, Cooper.
Mamiyaflex Camera Guide, Cooper.
Manual of Darkroom Procedures.
Medical & Dental Photog Guide, Tydings.
Minolta Guide, Tydings.
Minox Guide, Tydings.
Minox Guide, Amphoto.
Miranda Eye Level Reflex Guide, Tydings.
Mounting, Projecting and Storing Slides.
Nature Photography, Bennett.
Night Photography, Woolley.
Nikon F Eye Level Reflex Guide, Tydings.
Omega Enlarger Guide, Tydings.
120/620 Camera Guide, Arnold.
Outdoor Photography, Woolley.
Perfecting Your Enlarging, Gibson.
Petri Guide, Tydings.
Photo Darkroom Guide, Shumway.
Photo Darkroom Photog Guide, Amphoto.
Photographic Films & Their Uses, Woolley.
Photographic Make Up, Kehoe.
Photographic Print Quality, Procedures & Papers.
Photographing Children, Szasz.

Photographing Sports, Kauffman.
Photographing Women, Halmi.
Photographing Your Flowers, Roche.
Photography: Careers & Opportunities for You, Abel.
Photography Through Monoculars, Binoculars, Telescopes.
Polaroid Land Guide, Tydings.
Portrait Photography, Tydings.
Police & Crime Photography.
Praktina, Praktica, Pentacon, Edixaflex Guide.
Press & View Camera Technique, Wahl.
Printing with Variable Contrast Papers.
Retina Eye Level Reflex Guide, Tydings.
Retina Reflex Guide, Emanuel.
Retouching Negatives & Prints, West.
Ricoh Guide, Tydings.
Rolleiflex & Rolleicord Guide, Tydings.
Secrets of Successful Freelancing.
Single Lens Reflex Guide, Wahl.
Solar Enlarger Guide.
Star Gazing with Telescope & Camera.
Strobonar Electronic Flash Guide.
Sound for Your Color Movies.
Subminiature Techniques, Wahl.
Table Top & Still Life Phg., Bennett.
Tape Recorder Service & Trouble Shooting Workbook.
Tape Recording Guide, Marshall.
Telephoto & Wide Angle Photography, Simmons.
35mm Reference Guide, Pollack.
35mm Camera Rating Guide.
Teenagers Guide to Photography, Murphy.
Titling Your Own Color Movies.
Travel Photography Guide, Nettis.
Travel & Vacation Movie Guide.
Ultrablitz Guide, Tydings.
Voigtlander Guide, Tydings.
Voigtlander Bessamatic Guide.
Wedding & Party Photography.
Winning Photo Contests Guide.
Wollensak Lenses & Shutters.
Yashica Guide, Lowell.
Yashica Guide, Tydings.
Yashica Pentamatic Guide.
Zeiss Ikon Guide, Tydings.
Zone System Manual, White.

OF SPECIAL INTEREST . . .

All The Photo Tricks...............$4.95
Alpa Camera, Deschin................ 2.95
Applied Microscopy & Photomicrography.. 5.50
Artificial Light Photography, Adams.. 3.95
Audio Control Handbook, Oringel..... 6.95
Available Light & Your Camera, Wright.. 5.00
Build Your Own Enlarger............. 3.50
Child Photography Made Easy, Schneider.. 4.50
Close-ups & Copying in Color........ 2.95
Color: How to See & Use It, Bond.... 9.75
Contaflex Manual.................... 7.95
Creative 35mm Techniques, Woolley... 7.50
Creative Photographer, Feininger.... 5.95
Developing, Jacobson................ 4.50
Dictionary of Cinematography........ 4.95
Donovan on Child Portraiture........ 5.50
Electric Eye Movie Manual, Current.. 2.50
Electronic Flashlight Photography... 7.95
Encyclopedia of Colour Photography......12.50
Enlarging, Jacobson................. 4.50
Erith on Pictorial Photography...... 7.95
Exakta Manual....................... 9.95
Exposure, Berg...................... 5.00
Exposure Record, Adams. Ppr.$1.95; leather, 2.95
Feature Photos That Sell, Arnold.... 1.95
Filter Guide, Rothschild-Wright 2.50
Flash Photography, Parks 1.00
Floyd's Photo Tips.................. 2.50
Freelance Photographer's Handbook... 5.00
Fundamentals of Photographic Theory.. 7.50
Gevaert Manual of Photography,
  Craeybeck........................ 5.95
Glamour in Your Lens, MacGregor.... 2.50
Halsman on the Creation of
  Photographic Ideas 1.95
Handbook of Amateur Cinematography
  Vol. 2........................... 6.50
Hasselblad Photography, Barry....... 3.95
How I Photograph Nudes, Bunny Yeager.10.00
How to Develop, Print & Enlarge, Epstein 1.00
How to Develop, Print & Enlarge Your Own
  Pictures, Flynn.................. 5.95
How to Make Money in Photog., ppr....... 1.95
How to Pose the Model............... 4.95
How to Shoot a Movie Story, paper... 1.95
How to Shoot for Glamour, Bakal.... 2.95
How to Shoot Weddings, Arin........ 3.95
How to Take Better Home Movies, Gowland 2.50
How to Use Filters, Bates.......... 2.95
How to Use 8mm, Grossett........... 2.95
How to Use 16mm, Grossett.......... 2.95
How to Use Variable Contrast Papers,
  Jacobs........................... 2.50
Ilford Manual of Photography....... 6.50
Introduction to Cine, Postlethwaite. 3.50
Keppler on the Eye Level Reflex..... 4.95
Kodak Master Photoguide............. 1.95
Kodak Movie Photoguide............. 1.95
Leica Way 6.90
Lenses: How to Choose & Use Them, Russell 2.50

Lighting for Photography, Nurnberg.......... 5.00
Lighting for Portraiture, Nurnberg.......... 5.00
Linhof Practice.........................14.95
Lootens, on Enlarging................ 4.95
Minolta, Manual, Cooper 3.95
Minox Manual, Cooper................ 4.95
Miniature & Precision Cameras, Lipinsky.. 7.95
Model Art........................... 1.50
Modern Control in Photography....... 6.95
Modern Enlarging Technique.......... 3.50
More Colour Magic, W. Benser....... 4.50
Movie Making for Everyone........... 2.50
New York in Photographs............. 3.95
My Camera Pays Off, Sweet........... 4.95
My Ivory Cellar..................... 4.75
Natural Light Photography, Adams.... 3.95
Negative, The, Adams................ 3.95
Official Nikon 'F' Reflex Manual.... 2.50
Outer Space Photography, Paul....... 2.50
Pearlman on Print Quality........... 2.95
Photo Dictionary, Morgan, ppr....... 2.50
Photographic Lens Manual & Directory,
  cloth 3.50
Photographic Optics, Cox............ 5.75
Photographing Youth Manual.......... 2.50
Photography for Teenagers, Marshall. 3.95
Photography in Commerce and Industry,
  Faulkner-Taylor..................12.95
Photography: Its Materials & Processes..15.00
Photo Journalism.................... 5.95
Photo Oil Coloring for Fun & Profit. 4.25
Picture History of Photography, Pollack..22.50
Pilkington on Colour Photography....10.95
Portrait Photography................ 2.50
Portraits of Greatness, Karsh.......17.50
Practical Portrait Photography, Abel. 6.95
Print, The, Adams................... 3.95
Professional Methods for Amateur
  Photographers.................... 5.95
Reproduction of Colour..............12.95
Retina Handbook, Bomback 2.95
Retina Manual....................... 9.95
Retina Way, Croy.................... 5.95
Retina Reflex Way, Mannheim 7.50
Retouching, Croy.................... 4.50
Rollei Manual....................... 9.95
Rollei Way, Mannheim................ 6.95
Ski and Snow, Atkeson............... 8.50
Stereo Realist Manual, Morgan....... 2.95
Successful Color Photography, Feininger. 4.95
Successful Color Photography, Thompson 1.95
Successful Exposure Photography..... 1.95
Successful Flash Photography, Mannheim.. 1.95
Successful 35mm Photography, Matheson. 1.95
Successful Photography, Feininger.... 4.95
Summer's Children, Morgan........... 3.95
Table Tops & Titles in Color, Bombach. 2.95
Taking Colour Photographs........... 2.95
Taking Pictures After Dark, Satow... 2.50
35mm Picture Making, with Jouhar.... 7.95

35mm Photo Technique, Newcombe.......... 4.50
TV & Film Production Data Book, Pittaro 2.95
Ultra Miniature Photography, Cooper 3.95
Underwater Photography, Schenk & Kendall 3.50
U.S. Camera Annual, 61 & 63......... 6.75
  Each 3.50
Your A-Z Guide to Colour Photography... 5.50
Views to Dine By.................... 1.50
Writing for Television and Radio, Hilliard
Zoological Photography in Practice, Cott 12.50
35mm Negatives & Prints, Satow...... 2.50

(as long as they last)

Camera Touring Guide................ 1.00
Making Better Color Slides, Part 2.. 1.95
ACL Guide to Making Better Movies... 1.00

BASIC PHOTO SERIES by Ansel Adams
(Set of 4 Volumes)
#2—The Negative
#3—The Print
#4—Natural Light Photography
#5—Artificial Light Photography
each...... **$3.95**; set of 4 ...... **$14.25**
(NO DISCOUNT ON THIS OFFER

THE WORLD THROUGH MY EYES

(Continued from page 24)
position are important to my work. However, though my own work puts emphasis upon these qualities, I greatly admire certain other photographers' work that depends upon the use of softness and blur to express the intangibles of feeling and mood.

I believe that to accomplish anything worthwhile one must know and accept one's limitations and reject the temptation to exceed one's scope. Those who allow admiration for others' work to carry them beyond their own capacities no longer produce original work; they become mere imitators. Within one's own limitations, a personal style can be evolved through choice of subject and technique of rendition. The number of subjects to be photographed is limitless and the techniques of rendering are many. To encompass them all is impossible, and one must make a choice. Since no two people are alike, differences in personality will influence this choice. In following one's own way and pursuing one's own interests against the pressures and temptations to do otherwise, each finds his style. The discipline and dedication exacted in doing this, however, are so great that those who arrive at a highly personal style are few in relation to the total number of photographers. And fewer still are those whose talents are such that they create, through experiment in visual representation, a whole new way of seeing things. These few photographers, through their innovations, better the work of others and contribute to the advance of photography. And though their imitators may unfortunately be many, their own force is not canceled. Some of the photographers whom I admire and who have influenced my own thinking and work through their creativity are Erwin Blumenfeld, Ernst Haas, Gjon Mili, Laszlo Moholy-Nagy, Albert Renger-Patzsch, Eliot Porter, Man Ray, Emil Schulthess, W. Eugene Smith, and Edward Weston.

Each of these, dissatisfied with the accepted forms and rules of photographic expression, boldly struck out on his own. Each used existing but generally overlooked means and techniques to show familiar subjects in different ways, thereby making the observer aware of things that previously had escaped his attention or thought. In this way, each of these photographers created a powerful personal style.

When a photographer lacks a personal style, it is usually either because he is unimaginative or because he hasn't "found himself." As long as he is addicted to following the advice of others or is floundering in imitation, he cannot work out a style of his own.

What personal style I possess springs from a definite concept of the purpose of photography—of a "philosophy" which, briefly expressed, is this: Photography is a picture-language. Through it a photographer can communicate his ideas or feelings about people, events, or things.

To fulfill that purpose, a photograph must interest those for whom it is meant and must be presented in a form that the observer can understand.

The photographer's own true interest in his subject is very likely to call forth response in others. And if he has fully explored the possibilities of his subject, his picture is bound to appeal to others, for they will be caught by thought associations or similarity of feeling. Hundreds—thousands—of amateur photographers are proof of this in reverse: Free to spend their time in photographing things unassigned, with a chance to state their own ideas and express themselves completely, they instead endlessly take the most uninteresting subjects in stereotyped form, with the result that their pictures call forth no response in others. I am convinced that the work of many photographers would be tremendously improved if they restricted themselves to subjects in which they were really interested and photographed these for the sake of communication rather than merely to produce pictures.

Though the subject is of primary importance, inseparable from it is the form in which it is rendered. To decide upon the way in which a subject should be rendered—or translated—from reality into picture form is considerably more difficult than it may seem at first because a photograph is *not* a realistic reproduction, but a semiabstract rendition, of a subject. In consequence, its effect depends upon the use of symbols.

In photography, three-dimensional subjects must be rendered in two dimensions; motion must be expressed in a "still"; and in black-and-white renditions, color must be translated into shades of gray. Therefore, in this medium in which depth, motion, and color can only be suggested, symbols must be used, and only if they are selected and applied with skill and sensitivity will a photograph be good or excellent.

Anyone can take a recognizable picture of almost any subject, but there is a great difference between a merely recognizable and a truly effective rendition of the same subject. And whether a photograph falls into one category or the other is dependent upon the photographer's particular use of symbols. There are many symbols that can be used to suggest those qualities that cannot be rendered directly. Depth can be symbolized by perspective: apparent converging of receding parallel lines, and apparent diminution in size; foreshortening of form and overlapping of objects; by contrast between sharp and unsharp; or contrast between light and dark; and through composition. Motion can be symbolized by blur; multiple exposure or multiple printing; time exposure; panning; picture sequences; and through composition. And color can be symbolized by controlled contrast and graphically effective black and white. Symbols can furthermore be used to suggest intangibles: lightness and darkness, to suggest feeling or mood; graininess, to create emphasis through texture; halation, to give the intensity of light; and so forth.

Any subject or event can be photographed or presented in picture form in many different ways. Every change in distance; angle of view; focal length, angle, and coverage of the lens; speed, color-sensitivity, and graininess of the film; plane of focus; diaphragm aperture; filter color; film exposure; method of development; contrast of the printing paper; exposure, dodging, and cropping of the print; and every change in any one of a multitude of other factors will produce differences through combinations that are innumerable. Cartier-Bresson has had interesting things to say on the technique of catching the precise instant. Thorough knowledge of all these factors and techniques is required to express

(Continued on page 204)

How your camera can set you free long before retirement age

America's most successful child photographer was trapped in a job he hated until he discovered photography at 33. Today he lives and works in a luxurious suburban home paid for by his "hobby." Here is his advice to people interested in photography and bored with their jobs

By Harry Garfield

Do you ever have the feeling that you're trapped in your job for life?

That was how I felt until I was 33. Then something happened that changed the whole course of my life. It brought me such freedom and fulfillment that now I never want to quit what I'm doing.

I was a salesman — and hated it. Then one day I happened to take some pictures of my wife Helen with our old Brownie.

Looking back now, I realize the pictures were not especially good. But they got me excited about photography, and I started learning all I could about it. Then a friend asked me to photograph his child, and paid me for it. Soon I found myself working every weekend as a photographer, as one customer recommended me to another.

Finally my wife and I decided I should give up my job for photography. With the money we made photographing children at a resort that summer, we opened our first studio.

Since then I've had to enlarge my studio four times. I've won many prizes, and have had my pictures widely published in newspapers and magazines. I've been able to buy a home more luxurious than anything I ever dreamed of during my boyhood in an orphanage.

You can enjoy the same freedom I do

Can you do what I did? Can you start making pictures for pay in your spare time and gradually switch to full time? If you enjoy photography as much as I always have, I am positive you can. There are far more opportunities in photography today than when I started out. American business and the American public now demand some fifteen *million* professional photographs a year. There's no reason why you can't help supply this demand.

Proper professional training is important, however. Creative photography has made such startling advances, picture editors are no longer satisfied with "record" shots. They're always looking for that "magic difference" which marks the work of a really topnotch pro.

Learn the "magic difference" from men who have achieved it

I've often wished there were some way I could help people with ambitions in photography get the kind of training they need.

I found the answer several years ago. Victor Keppler asked me to join nine of the most famous men in photography to create an entirely new kind of home-study school — the Famous Photographers School.

We spent three years pouring into a series of remarkable lessons all the know-how it had taken us many years in photography to acquire. Sometimes we found ourselves in complete agreement on the best way to handle a common photographic problem. At other times one of us would contribute a prized studio secret that the rest of us had never known.

Course eye-opening even to us

By this sharing and dovetailing of everything we had learned in our own careers, we developed lessons for the Course which opened up new vistas in creative photography that were exciting even to us.

To drive these lessons home, we then devised a series of assignments which you can carry out in your own home or neighborhood, using your own camera.

Each set of negatives and prints you send in as part of your assignments is analyzed by one of our instructors, himself a skilled professional photographer supervised by the ten of us who started the School. Through detailed visual critiques of your pictures — covering everything from basic techniques to composition, timing, mood, and artistic conception — your instructor shows you precisely how to turn those pictures into distinguished professional photographs. Then he "talks" to you by dictaphone — giving you, in a long friendly letter, both the praise you deserve and the constructive criticism you need. And he guides you toward the fields and markets for which you display the greatest talent.

In this way, lesson by lesson, you systematically develop your photographic skill, perception, and creativity to meet the highest professional standards. You learn to use your camera so instinctively that both seeing and

---

---

capturing great photographs becomes second nature to you.

I see my story happening all over again

This new approach to photographic training is already showing impressive results. Recently we received a letter from a student which especially pleased me — it reminded me so much of my own beginning days.

"When I enrolled," writes T. W. Himes, who works for Sunkist Growers in Houston, Texas, "my goal was to take a '10-year early retirement' from Sunkist at 55 and spend all my energies on photography. You'll be glad to know I'm already on my way."

When Mr. Himes was on his third lesson, a large Southwestern industry invited him to photograph one of their plants. "Much to my delight," he reports, "most of the exposures came out beautifully, and resulted in an order for 32 prints. These were used in brochures and will result in re-orders as well as additional new work." Since starting our Course, Mr. Himes also has been commissioned by his employer to take sales promotion photographs, has had his work published in the *Houston Chronicle*, and has been building a successful part-time portrait business.

Send for 48-page book about Course

If you would like to be free to lead a better life long before retirement age, getting paid for work you love—send for our 48-page booklet. It describes our Course, how it operates, and what it can do for you. The coupon below will bring you a copy without obligation.

WHO IS THAT?
By Robert Riger

(Continued from page 83) rapher. So I became an artist-photographer, and when I added the research material and field notes and conversations with the athletes I became a writer. This is what I do. I am a reporter, a journalist. There is no art involved as a conscious, applied thing.

This year, after eleven years of free lance work previously with *Sports Illustrated* and *Esquire* and many books, I closed my studio to join the American Broadcasting Co. as artist-reporter on ABC's Wide World of Sport. I now use my drawings to preview an event—to show the viewer what to look for—and photographs for analysis after the event. I have joined a staff of experts in various sports on camera and report as a commentator as well. I'm convinced, for a picture man, television is the only journalism today.

I believe in the intense mental energy of an athlete. I take his physical strength for granted. If I can touch the pulse beat of his thinking in a look or a gesture, entering his world and suspending that instant in time with a sketch or a photograph, then I've done the job.

If an athlete poses he leaves his world mentally and enters mine and you get bubble gum cards. The photographer who asks someone to come to his studio so he may photograph them does so because of his own ego and the sitter's, or because his business is make-believe. Being a studio photographer seems to me to be a dull life. You've got to move out.

The world is a great picture. The texture of each land of each day of all people moving through a moment of their lives is a great picture—if you see it just right. I travel more than 60,000 miles a year and I would go batty sitting home.

In documentary photography you may be fully aware of this picture and photograph it or you may be moved by the spirit of what you see and photograph it and find you have recorded a great picture. The picture is there always and you put it on the film as it is. You do not make it. This is the difference: a painter makes his picture—a photographer copies his. A photographer with more imagination will copy it more imaginatively but a painter will have the world copy him. He creates it.

The documentary is a true art form, perhaps the only one in photography. I take many pictures to achieve it and yet the universality in one picture or in each picture is the key to it, and this is the paradox. As in painting, the documentary picture must transcend the actual fact; in football or horse racing or boxing it must be a record of a specific game and player and of all games and all players too. It must be significant and so it is not "candid" photography or trick photography or news photography "shot" under specific assignment with limitations. It must be entirely free in its choice of approach and the mood achieved must not be the mood of the photographer but of this world he is documenting—and the intensity of the people moving through a moment of their lives—whether they be fishermen, soldiers, or football players, will establish the impact. The light will establish the drama. What the photographer does creatively is see this world he is looking at in a certain light and he puts this on film. Light becomes his personal choice in black and white or in color to sustain a mood throughout an entire story so that the story can be understood anywhere by anyone and have meaning.

The so-called technical aspects of photography are quite simple. Exposure is a personal choice to put just so much light on the film. (This is why we squint at a choice subject—adjusting the light so it is just the way we want it. The trick is to get your camera to squint just right and then develop the film to hold this light quality.) I have never used an exposure meter. There is no time for it in sports. You must smell the light. I believe if there is any "talent" necessary in photography it is the art of judging existing light—instantly. From the full accidental negative you then personally choose that area for the print as you remembered your subject. I take the picture, develop it, edit and print it myself. It's like baking a cake—you can't have six people in on it.

I use 9 different cameras, but only one kind of film—Tri X. (Kodachrome II for color.) The two factors that determine the cameras to be used are the teams that are playing and the weather. In football the particular offense of the team playing dictates the camera to be used because of maneuverability and angle. Most sports photographers use the same equipment on all sporting events and this I feel is their misfortune. Some cameras are, of necessity, bad weather cameras and have to be used in rain or snow and impossibly bad light. The cameras I use most frequently are the 70mm high speed Hulcher sequence and Japanese 35mm Pentax and Nikon with German, not Japanese, lenses. I have a habit of mixing the pieces of 4 or 5 cameras together to achieve a certain result. You almost have to design your own camera to do a specific job. On an average Sunday I take more than 800 pictures and for many of the key pro football games I will shoot 1100 or more. There's a great chance for equipment failure even though it's thoroughly checked out before a game and secondary cameras must be brought into action. It stands to reason that if you see the world in your light and you expose it that way—most of your negatives should be the same density and printed on the same grade paper which is the rule in my case.

Photography is a miracle, a phenomenon, a delight. The current fad of calling photography a fine art is bunk. How can a man's efforts of a hundred hours be compared with another man's of 1/100th of a second? How can they say the results are the same. Painting and sculpture, draftsmanship is work. Photography is play—a wonderful game.

Documentary photography in sport is simply a matter of intelligence and marksmanship. The excitement alone sustains me. I believe every artist should have a concept of life. If it is universal and clear and intensified by a personal style, the art is good—maybe even significant. My concept is dramatic, my style is the documentary. My subject is sports. It gives me an honest world to document dramatically.

YOU CAN'T BEAT GENERAL ELECTRIC FOR CREATIVE LIGHTING

Ringmaster Don Mohler turns another tough lighting problem into a stellar act!

Quit juggling lights! Control lighting the Gee-Easy way with G-E AG-1 Flashbulbs!

Don't juggle! Don't struggle! It's easy to shoot fine quality pictures of people, babies, tabletops...even executive portraits. The secret is to get a good basic lighting ratio between your key light and your fill light. How? Use a General Electric AG-1 blue-bulb at the camera for fill—and a General Electric AG-1 clear flash bulb 45° off camera on an extension cord as your key light. Just be sure that you place both lamps at the same distance lamp-to-subject. Simple! Always bear in mind that clear flash puts out quite a bit more light than blue. So use it to its fullest advantage for speed, simplicity, ease and uniform results. Any more tough lighting problems? Just call on Don Mohler at General Electric, Nela Park, Cleveland 12, Ohio for information about creative lighting.

THE WORLD THROUGH MY EYES

(Continued from page 200)

precisely what one wishes to communicate.

A good photograph, I think, is one which conveys to the observer something that he has not seen, known, or thought of before; in other words, a photograph which is "new" to him, insofar as it stimulates his imagination, increases his knowledge, or enriches him aesthetically, intellectually, or emotionally.

This demands a great deal from the photographer. The kind of newness I have in mind is that which results from an original approach or from an innovation—a new way of seeing or rendering a subject; that which proves to be the successful end of a search for a new way of expression; that which extends the artist's vision; that which the creative photographer seeks and finds; and, finally, that which the photographer is able to extract from the seemingly implacable structure of technique to convey what he wishes to say. For in creative hands, the camera, like the telescope and the microscope, becomes an instrument to widen man's horizons—providing greater knowledge, understanding, and insight.

This kind of newness demands a thorough comprehension of the characteristics of the photographic medium and a utilization of those qualities that belong to no other.

FRANK COWAN

(Continued from page 148)

and his so-called *uneasiness*, quite charming.

He informed me that he gained great satisfaction out of solving problems, not necessarily photographic ones, but all kinds. And, one of his biggest problems, and one that he finds the most exciting and challenging of all is becoming the owner of a former Con Edison power plant—which he is converting into a fabulous studio. This time consuming project is located on Sixth Street off First Avenue and runs through from one block to the other. Originally a ten-story building, it will be divided into four floors. There is enough space behind the building to accommodate a parking lot, inside there is a hoisting crane that can literally float an automobile in space from the ceiling. The size of the roof is tremendous and Frank unblinkingly says, "It would make a great restaurant." There is so much space that he's not quite sure what he'll do with all of it. But on second thought, "We can always find some kind of use for it."

This vital young man, who is also an expert on American Antiques and collects oriental rugs, was married a-year-and-a-half ago. "She," says Cowan, "is my direct opposite, she is studying for her Ph.D. at the University of Columbia and she makes up for the deficiency on my side."

This deficient fellow has also become quite knowledgeable in the ways of heating, plumbing and architectural design and to top it all off—he and a collaborator are busy completing a black and white movie on weekends which will run about twenty-five minutes.

As I said goodbye, Bette brought in a toy rocket, a prop to be used in a toothpaste ad—my imagination ran wild but in the end it all added up to my undoubtedly switching to his client's brand.

Four of the black and white pictures that appear in his portfolio were done on assignment. The fifth, page 150 of the grimacing young lady, was done for fun and was a good match for Cowan's photo on the opposite page which was shot for the American Machine & Foundry Company. Page 149 shows copy writer Ed Valenti doubling as a father in a diaper ad for Chix Diapers. These three pictures were taken with a Rollei. Page 152, photo of mouse held in hand was shot with a Hasselblad for the Cancer Society. The cat, page 153, was made for Johnson Wax to show sparkle and durability of a floor. Mamiyaflex camera.

Subscribe

Now To "Photography's Solid Three"

1 U.S. Camera
2 Camera 35
3 Better Home Movie Making

1

U.S. CAMERA—a complete photography magazine for the amateur, whether he is a beginner or an expert. Each monthly issue has how-to-do-it articles on every phase of photography, from snapping the picture to printing it; columns interestingly written by experts in their field on such subjects as 35mm, color, darkroom, movies, sound, techniques; latest developments in equipment; creative and technical approaches suggested, and illustrated with fine pictures. U.S. Camera is your key to a more rewarding hobby.

1 Year $5.00

When writing advertisers please say you saw it in U. S. CAMERA ANNUAL

2

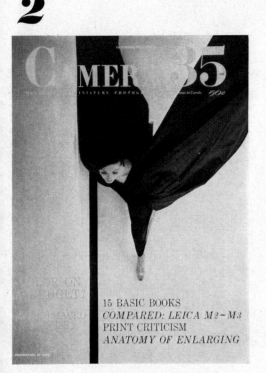

15 BASIC BOOKS
COMPARED: *LEICA M2-M3*
PRINT CRITICISM
ANATOMY OF ENLARGING

CAMERA 35—the bi-monthly for those knowledgeable 35mm enthusiasts who demand a fine magazine devoted exclusively to miniature photography. CAMERA 35 offers, besides comprehensive technical articles, stories on various other aspects of photography to delight the hobbyist who enjoys reading, purely for pleasure, about his favorite subject. These may encompass art, humor, philosophy, and history. Photographs are always superb examples of the work of ace exponents of this medium.

1 Year $2.50

3

BETTER HOME MOVIE MAKING is invaluable to the amateur moviemaker in teaching him to make interesting, imaginative and technically perfect home movies. Each bi-monthly issue a meaty package of how-to-do-it articles, lessons, scripts, columns to show how to *make*, not merely *take* movies. Master the art and technique of lighting, editing, directing; learn about close-ups, dissolves, special effects, films, lenses, exposures, new equipment. Enter the annual Cine Circle Contest! Increase your proficiency with every issue.

1 Year $2.50

Bunny Yeager's New, Exciting Book
free "HOW I PHOTOGRAPH NUDES"

Authoress Bunny Yeager

...with your first selection to reveal the unique advantages of membership in

START YOUR MEMBERSHIP
WITH ANY ONE OF THESE VALUABLE BOOKS

THE DELIGHTS OF PHOTOGRAPHY by Giorgina Reid
A working manual for every member of the family. Illustrated by more than 170 photos. List Price $5.95
Member's Price $5.35

PHOTOGRAPHING THE NUDE by Lewis Tulchin
The principles that lead to successful photography of the nude. Illustrated by more than 100 figure studies. List Price $10.00
Member's Price $7.95

STROBE—THE LIVELY LIGHT by Howard Luray
Every possible application of electronic flash for black-and-white and color. Over 120 illustrations. List Price $5.95
Member's Price $5.35

CREATIVE 35MM TECHNIQUES by A. E. Wooley
A thorough and informative manual of all uses of the 35mm camera. Over 150 illustrations. List Price $7.50
Member's Price $5.95

THE COMPLETE BOOK OF NATURE PHOTOGRAPHY by Russ Kinne
Methods, equipment and know-how on photographing nature subjects. Over 140 photographs. List Price $7.50
Member's Price $5.95

The Camera Arts Book Club

Thousands of camera enthusiasts, from casual "shutter bugs" to discerning professionals, have found this invaluable book club stimulating in many ways. Selections are authentic, profusely illustrated and clearly written to help you shoot better pictures, improve techniques, add to your fun or profit. Each month you will be offered books on figure and glamour photography, color, composition, lighting, exposure, films, lenses, retouching, movie-making, child photography, national and international annuals, etc. Each book is carefully selected by qualified editors and consultants. Stop wasting precious time and money searching and paying full prices for the books you want when The Camera Arts Book Club brings you these same books at UP TO 40% OFF LIST PRICE!

Mail this Coupon Now!

THE CAMERA ARTS BOOK CLUB · 151-51 Seventh Ave., Whitestone 57, N. Y. IP-65

Please enroll me as a charter member of THE CAMERA ARTS BOOK CLUB. Send me the selection I have checked and my FREE VOLUME of Bunny Yeager's "How I Photograph Nudes." Forthcoming selections and alternates will be described to me in a monthly advance Bulletin and I may decline any book by simply returning the printed form always provided. I agree to buy as few as four additional selections (or alternates) at the reduced Member's Price (plus a small shipping charge) during the next twelve months, and I may resign at any time thereafter.

NAME _____

ADDRESS _____

CITY _____ ZONE_____ STATE_____

☐ Enclosed $_____   ☐ Bill my account

☐ If under 21, have parent sign here_____

☐ THE DELIGHTS OF PHOTOGRAPHY
☐ PHOTOGRAPHING THE NUDE
☐ STROBE—THE LIVELY LIGHT
☐ CREATIVE 35MM TECHNIQUES
☐ THE COMPLETE BOOK
    OF NATURE PHOTOGRAPHY

Note: Offer applies to U.S., Possessions and Canada only. Foreign memberships must be accompanied by an advance deposit of $10.

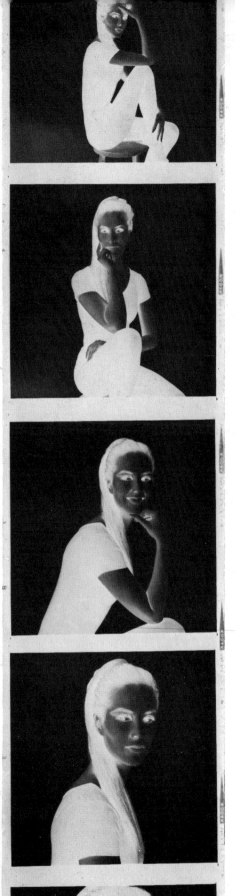

These 5 negatives
were all shot with
a twin-lens reflex
at the same distance
on the same roll.

How?

With a Mamiya twin-lens reflex
and 5 interchangeable lenses!

Mamiya C series cameras are the world's only twin-lens reflexes with
completely interchangeable lenses. Focal lengths range from 65mm
wide angle to 180mm telephoto. See your dealer or write for details.
MAMIYA division of Ehrenreich Photo-Optical Industries, Inc.
111 Fifth Avenue, New York 3, New York, Dept. US-65

Always what you expect them to be...

There is one big fact about all Kodak color films: you can count on top quality and dependability roll after roll. Choose KODACHROME II Film for sharpest detail and lifelike color . . . KODACHROME-X for more speed and contrast . . . KODAK EKTACHROME-X Film for vivid color . . . High Speed EKTACHROME for action and low light . . . or sharp, high-latitude KODACOLOR Film for prints and enlargements. You can shoot with confidence, because you know the films will always be what you

EASTMAN KODAK COMPANY
Rochester, N. Y.